ADLARD COLES CLASSIC BOAT SERIES

Lofting a Boat

A step-by-step manual

ADLARD COLES CLASSIC BOAT SERIES

Lofting a Boat

A step-by-step manual

Roger Kopanycia

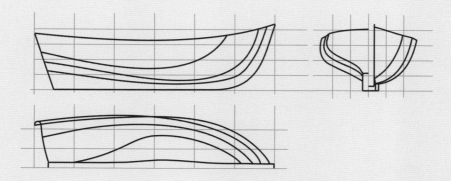

ADLARD COLES

ADLARD COLES
Bloomsbury Publishing Plc
50 Bedford Square, London WC1B 3DP
29 Earlsfort Terrace, Dublin 2, Ireland

ADLARD COLES NAUTICAL, ADLARD COLES and the Buoy logo are
trademarks of Bloomsbury – www.adlardcoles.com

First edition published 2011
8 10 9

Print ISBN 978-1-4081-3112-1
ePub ISBN 978-1-4729-0763-9
ePDF ISBN 978-1-4081-5129-7

A CIP catalogue record for this book is available from the British Library.

This book is produced using paper that is made from wood grown in
managed, sustainable forests. It is natural, renewable and recyclable.
The logging and manufacturing processes conform to the environmental
regulations of the country of origin.

Typeset in 10pt Rotis Sans
Printed and bound in India by Replika Press Pvt. Ltd.

Note: while all reasonable care has been taken in the publication of this
book, the publisher takes no responsibility for the use of the methods or
products described in the book.

CONTENTS

INTRODUCTION

Lofting has been called an art, a science, technical/engineering drawing and also a form of magic and mysticism, but what's it really all about? Basically, it's the process of creating a series of 'full-size' drawings of a boat to allow it to be accurately and successfully constructed either by yourself or a boatyard. For many people, the thought of lofting a boat strikes them with fear, or they think it's beyond their ability.

The aim of this book is to encourage anyone to have a go at lofting, by setting out a range of techniques that will work for any boat. It doesn't matter if you want to loft a 12 foot sailing dinghy, a 20 foot motor cruiser or a 60 foot deep-keeled, ocean-going yacht – the range of skills and techniques are exactly the same; the only real difference is the size of the finished boat.

Originally trained as an engineer and now a qualified teacher, I've worked as a lofting and boatbuilding instructor for over ten years, and have successfully passed on the skills and techniques needed to confidently loft a boat to hundreds of students.

Lofting is a visual activity and I can't understand why so many books (with a few notable exceptions) use lots of words but very few drawings. Hopefully, this book is the other way round: lots of drawings but not too many words. There's a small glossary at the back, however, covering some of the basic terms you'll need.

The book is divided into two parts. Part 1 develops the range of core skills and techniques used in lofting and is arranged as a series of step-by-step drawings guiding you through every stage of the lofting process. It's exactly the same method I've used over the years with all of the students I've been fortunate enough to work with and teach. The book starts at the very beginning, with a blank loft floor, and looks at setting out the Lofting Grid, followed by the lofting process itself, which ends with the full-size reproduction of the boat's Lines Drawing. These core skills are at the very heart of lofting and are fundamental to all of the work that will be done in Part 2.

Part 2 deals with the techniques used to transform a full-size Lines Drawing into a construction drawing, which then allows us to take templates and Mould Stations off the loft floor. It also covers more involved aspects of lofting such as Stem-Bevel development (ie creating the cross-sectional size and shape of the Stem at any point around its curve) and the development/ expansion of a Radiused Transom (on both its forward and aft face). As with Part 1, all of the techniques needed to achieve the end result are shown as a series of step-by-step drawings.

As with so many things in life, where there is rarely one single definitive way to carry out a task, lofting issues usually have a wealth of solutions. We all have opinions on the best way to get a job done, and the techniques described in this book are no exception. But all of the techniques and methods shown here have been used to successfully teach hundreds of students how to loft a boat.

Please visit my website at www.streamandshore.com, which has details of the lofting courses and one-to-one training that I can provide anywhere in the world to suit your needs.

Finally, I'd like to thank all of the people who have encouraged me over the years to write this book, but in particular Allyn Burton and Olly Hodgson for their help in trialling the final draft, my brother Garry for his ability to look at the book from a layman's point of view, and finally Claire for her limitless patience and understanding.

PART ONE

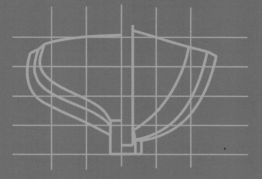

WHAT IS LOFTING?

Lofting is the process of drawing, or 'laying down', a boat, full size, in three different views, using information found in a Lines Drawing (a small-scale drawing of the boat) and an Offset Table (a table of measurements either created by the designer or taken from an original boat). These three views are:

The Profile View

A view of the boat from the side (ie its Profile) drawn onto a grid of horizontal Waterlines (WL) and vertical Station Lines (Stn).

The Body Plan

A series of vertical cross-sections through the hull drawn at the 'Stations'. As a boat is typically symmetrical about its centreline (C/L), we'd usually only draw in half of each Station cross-section.

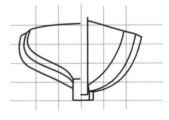

The Half–breadth or Waterline View

A series of horizontal cross-sections through the hull at designated Waterlines.

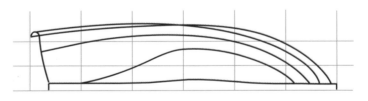

As well as these views, there will also be the Buttock Lines (drawn in the Profile View) and the Diagonals (typically drawn below the Half-breadth View). Both of these lines, as you'll see later on, are used to check and correct the 'fairness' of any previously drawn lines so that the finished boat is as accurate as possible.

WHY BOTHER LOFTING A BOAT?

Lofting a boat before starting to build can have many advantages for the enthusiast and the professional alike. The range of boats to build is much larger, as most of the old classic yachts and motorboats will not come with a set of plans containing full-size frames etc, making lofting the only option. The process of lofting also involves fairing the lines and then making any necessary corrections until all of the lines in all of the views correspond to one another. This will ultimately lead to a boat which is not only as accurately drawn as possible, but also pleasing to the eye. Remember, a boat can outlast most of us, so it helps if it looks good!

In these days of CAD and plans, where the Body Plan has been drawn full size and other information supplied as a scaled or dimensioned drawing, it's tempting to forget about lofting the boat and just get on with building it. While there's nothing wrong with doing this, lofting a boat gives us the opportunity to correct any errors in the Offset Table or Lines Drawing which may have accidentally occurred at the drafting stage. It also helps when the time comes to pick up all of the constructional information needed to build the Backbone or make the Mould Stations.

The process of lofting also gives us a better understanding of the finished boat, as we've been involved from the very beginning. The sense of satisfaction and achievement involved in successfully lofting a boat from scratch cannot be underestimated.

THE LINES DRAWING AND OFFSET TABLE

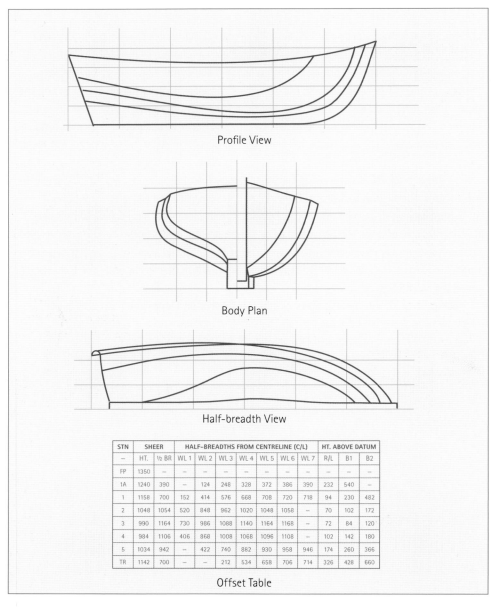

Profile View

Body Plan

Half-breadth View

STN	SHEER		HALF-BREADTHS FROM CENTRELINE (C/L)							HT. ABOVE DATUM		
–	HT.	½ BR	WL 1	WL 2	WL 3	WL 4	WL 5	WL 6	WL 7	R/L	B1	B2
FP	1350	–	–	–	–	–	–	–	–	–	–	–
1A	1240	390	–	124	248	328	372	386	390	232	540	–
1	1158	700	152	414	576	668	708	720	718	94	230	482
2	1048	1054	520	848	962	1020	1048	1058	–	70	102	172
3	990	1164	730	986	1088	1140	1164	1168	–	72	84	120
4	984	1106	406	868	1008	1068	1096	1108	–	102	142	180
5	1034	942	–	422	740	882	930	958	946	174	260	366
TR	1142	700	–	–	212	534	658	706	714	326	428	660

Offset Table

The layout of the Lines Drawing and Offset Table will usually look something like this, although hull shapes will vary depending upon the design and style, with the views of the boat and a table of offsets (measurements) which will be used to plot the full-size lines on the loft floor. In general, the 'offsets' will typically be a measurement from the centreline (C/L) 'out' and a measurement from a Datum or Waterline either 'up' or 'down'. The measurements can either be in imperial or metric.

Next we'll look at an Offset Table in greater detail. It's always a good idea to try and look at a range of Lines Drawings and Offset Tables to see how the designer has laid out the boat and the information. Note that when taking or using measurements from the Offset Table, they're only used once, so it's a good idea to put a line through them as you go so that they won't accidentally be used again.

STN	SHEER		HALF-BREADTHS FROM CENTRELINE (C/L)							HT. ABOVE DATUM		
—	HT.	H.BR	WL 1	WL 2	WL 3	WL 4	WL 5	WL 6	WL 7	R/L	B1	B2
FP	4/5/1+	—	—	—	—	—	—	—	—	—	—	—
1A	4/0/6	1/3/3	—	0/4/7	0/9/6	1/0/7+	1/2/5	1/3/2-	1/3/3	0/9/1	1/9/2	—
1	3/9/4	2/3/4	0/6/0	1/4/2	1/10/5	2/2/2	2/3/7	2/4/3-	2/4/2+	0/3/6	0/9/0+	1/7/0-
2	3/5/2	3/5/4	1/8/4	1/9/7	3/1/7	3/4/1+	3/5/2	3/5/5	—	0/2/6	0/4/0	0/6/6
3	3/3/0	3/9/7	2/4/6	3/2/7	3/6/7-	3/8/7	3/9/7	3/10/0	—	0/2/7-	0/3/2+	0/4/6
4	3/2/6	3/7/1	1/4/0	2/10/1	3/3/5	3/6/1-	3/7/1+	3/7/5	—	0/4/0	0/5/5	0/7/1-
5	3/4/5+	3/1/1	—	1/4/5	2/5/1	3/10/6	3/0/5	3/1/6	3/1/2	0/6/7	0/10/2	1/2/3
TR	3/8/7	2/3/4	—	—	0/8/3	1/9/0	2/1/7	2/3/6+	2/4/1	1/0/7-	1/4/7	2/2/0-

Above is a typical 'imperial' Offset Table, where the measurements are in feet, inches and 8ths of an inch. Taking Stn 2-WL 5 as an example, 3/5/2 = 3ft, 5in and $\frac{2}{8}$ of an inch. Some measurements have a '+' or '-' sign after the last number: this is to show that when plotted onto the loft floor we add or subtract a little bit from the last number.

STN	SHEER		HALF-BREADTHS FROM CENTRELINE (C/L)							HT. ABOVE DATUM		
—	HT.	½ BR	WL 1	WL 2	WL 3	WL 4	WL 5	WL 6	WL 7	R/L	B1	B2
FP	1350	—	—	—	—	—	—	—	—	—	—	—
1A	1240	390	—	124	248	328	372	386	390	232	540	—
1	1158	700	152	414	576	668	708	720	718	94	230	482
2	1048	1054	520	848	962	1020	1048	1058	—	70	102	172
3	990	1164	730	986	1088	1140	1164	1168	—	72	84	120
4	984	1106	406	868	1008	1068	1096	1108	—	102	142	180
5	1034	942	—	422	740	882	930	958	946	174	260	366
TR	1142	700	—	—	212	534	658	706	714	326	428	660

The table above is a typical 'metric' Offset Table, with the measurements all in mm, rounded up or down to the nearest mm. On a larger yacht, a metric Offset Table may be in metres: for example, 3.785m. It doesn't really matter which system is used as long as it is clear to the person lofting the boat.

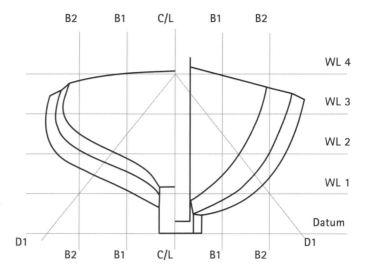

STN	Diagonals	
–	D1	D2
1	1/6/0	2/7/0
2	1/11/2	3/2/3
3	2/2/2	3/4/2
4	2/3/2	3/5/4
5	2/2/3	3/4/7
TR	1/11/4	2/5/6

As well as the typical Offset Tables shown previously, some boats may have a set of 'Diagonal' offsets. These will look similar to the table shown above left. A Diagonal is different to the other offsets because the measurement shown in the table is measured from the centre point of a line drawn at a position determined by the designer. A typical Diagonal is shown in the drawing above. In this example, the designer has stated that the Diagonal starts on the C/L at WL 4 and passes through B2 and WL 1 – any Diagonal measurements from the Offset Table would be along this line. The Diagonal is drawn to measurements set by the designer. It extends both sides of the C/L in the Body Plan. We'll look at the use of these Diagonal offsets when we plot the Stations in the Body Plan.

Depending on the designer or client, the Lines Drawing and Offset Table may be to either the 'outside' or 'inside' of the hull planking. The important thing to remember is that the techniques used to loft the boat are exactly the same; you will just need to work with the information given by the designer. Given the choice, I prefer it if a boat's offsets are to the outside of the hull planking, as I can then loft the boat and decide on any changes in hull thickness afterwards. For the rest of this book, unless stated otherwise, the offset measurements and lines drawn will be to the outside of the hull.

HOW MUCH SPACE DO I NEED TO LOFT A BOAT?

This is one of the more common questions I've been asked by students. The short answer is 'as large a space as possible', but obviously it must be at least as long as the maximum length of the boat and usually as wide as the maximum beam. For example, taking a yacht which is 30ft long and has a beam of 10ft and a height from the base of the Keel to the Sheer of 9ft, it would be possible to loft it in a space about 32–35ft long by about 10–12ft wide, but the various views of the boat would all have to be overlaid on top of each other. Even if we were to use a range of different coloured pens, the final lofting drawing would be very confusing. It would be far better to have a space greater than 35ft long and about 25ft wide so that most, if not all, of the views of the boat could be drawn in a separate area. This would be even more important when it came to using the final lofting to draw in and pick up the shapes of construction Moulds and templates for the Stem, Keel, Sternpost, Transom etc.

Apart from the space needed simply to loft the boat, the more space that's available the easier it will be to check that the line that's just been plotted is truly 'fair to the eye'. This is one of the most important – if not *the* most important – things to bear in mind when lofting because, as we'll see later on, it's no good just slavishly taking the offset measurements, plotting them on the loft floor and then joining them together with a batten. It's more important to achieve a line that's fair to the eye, even if that means missing out one or more of the measurements taken from the Offset Table. As mentioned previously, an offset measurement should only be used once – if we then have to ignore a measurement to get a fair line, the next time we need to use that point it will be the fair line measurement, not the offset measurement, that will be picked up and transferred.

TOOLS FOR THE JOB

You've decided on the boat, the loft floor has been sorted out and you're ready to start. Years ago most lofting was carried out using French chalk on a black-painted floor, but now we generally use pencils and/or pens on boards of MDF or Masonite secured onto the loft floor and painted white. If the finished lofting is going to be shipped to a client, then it is possible to loft the boat onto paper or drafting film to make shipping easier and much cheaper.

TOOLS REQUIRED (IN NO PARTICULAR ORDER):

1 Offset Table, Lines Drawing and construction drawing

2 String line or chalk line

3 Straight edge

4 Trammels or large compass

5 Pencils and sharpener

6 Tape measure and/or long ruler

7 'Tick stick'/lifting batten (used to pick up and transfer a 'measurement' from one view to another)

8 Large set square or builder's square

9 A selection of 'fairing battens' (ideally both wooden and plastic) of varying lengths, but ideally as long as possible

10 A selection of 'ship's curves' – not essential but can be useful for blending one curve into another

11 Hammer and nails

12 Spline/lofting weights

13 Eraser and 'eraser shield' (very useful later on)

THE LOFTING PROCEDURE

We're going to be lofting a round-bilged boat with a flat, 'raked' Transom, and the first thing to do is to set out the Lofting Grid onto the loft floor. When the Lofting Grid has been finished we can look at the actual procedure we are going to use to loft the boat. The first five lines to be drawn onto the Lofting Grid are: the Sheerline, Profile Line and Rabbetline (all in the Profile View), followed by the Rabbetline and the Sheerline (in the Half-breadth or Waterline View). Once these lines have been 'faired' (even if it means ignoring one or more of the measurements from the Offset Table) they become 'fixed', defining the overall size and shape of the boat.

Following this, the rest of the lines and views will be plotted in the following order:

1   Station Lines plotted in the Body Plan*

2   Waterlines plotted in the Half-breadth or Waterline View

3   Buttocks plotted in the Profile View

4   Diagonals plotted to check the fairness of all the other lines

5   The development/expansion of the Transom and the Deck Camber

* Why do we plot Station Lines before Waterlines?

As you will see shortly, Station Lines are plotted using either two or three sets of information, depending on the design, whereas Waterlines are plotted using a single source of information. Therefore, if the Station Lines are plotted and faired first, they are more likely to give us a fair Waterline, but the same cannot be said if we do them the other way round.

SETTING OUT THE LOFTING GRID

The information needed to set out the Lofting Grid (and loft the boat itself) can be found in the Offset Table and the Lines Drawing. Note that the spacing distance of the Waterlines, Station Lines and Buttocks doesn't have to be equal: every boat will be different. The important thing is to spend a little time studying the information *before* starting to loft the boat; this time will never be wasted and can actually save time later on.

Step 1 (of 12)

1   Set out the Datum, Baseline or LWL/DWL (the term Datum will be used, mostly, for consistency) using a tightly stretched string line/chalk line held at the ends with nails.

2   Using the straight edge, mark the line onto the loft floor with a pencil.

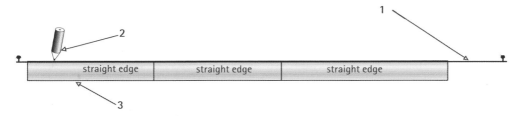

3   Overlap the straight edge when you pencil in the Datum Line: this prevents any 'staggering' of the line, as we can use the previous part of the line as a reference for the next part.

Step 2

When the Datum Line is in place, mark out the position of the FP (forward perpendicular, sometimes called Station 0), AP (aft perpendicular), all the Station Lines (for the Profile/Sheer View) and the positions of the C/L (centreline) and Buttock Lines (for the Body Plan).

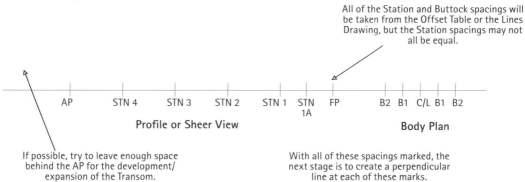

All of the Station and Buttock spacings will be taken from the Offset Table or the Lines Drawing, but the Station spacings may not all be equal.

If possible, try to leave enough space behind the AP for the development/ expansion of the Transom.

With all of these spacings marked, the next stage is to create a perpendicular line at each of these marks.

Step 3

We now need to create a perpendicular line for all of the marks on the Datum Line, using either trammels (see right) or a large drawing compass.

1   With the pencil in hole 1, place the point onto one of the marks (in this case, Stn 3) and then draw two arcs either side of the Station (x). If using a compass, set it to about a quarter of its maximum span.

2   Repeat this process for all of the 'marks' along the Datum Line (FP, AP, Stations, C/L and Buttocks).

X   X
STN 3   STN 2

Step 4

We now need to move the pencil from hole 1 and put it in hole 2 – if using a compass, open it out as far as possible.

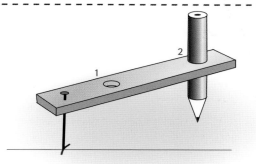

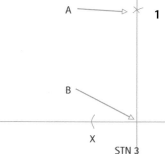

1   Place the trammel/compass point onto one of the marks (x) and draw a large arc. Repeat this process from the other point; we should then have two arcs that intersect at points A and C.

A
B
X   X
STN 3   STN 2

C

2   Using a straight edge, join up the three points A, B and C. We now have a line which is truly perpendicular to the Datum Line.

3   Repeat this process for all of the marks (FP, AP, Stations, C/L and Buttocks) along the Datum Line.

Step 5

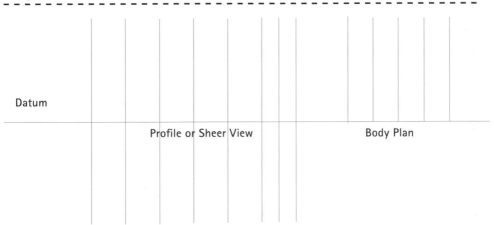

With all of the perpendicular lines drawn in, the grid should look something like this. We're now ready to draw in the Waterlines (see Step 6). There's no need to project the perpendicular lines below the Datum in the area of the Body Plan, as this space will not be used.

(Note: Station 1A was inserted to show that Stations do not need to be equally spaced – it will no longer form part of this book.)

Step 6

From information in the Lines Drawing or the Offset Table, mark out the vertical spacing of the Waterlines relative to the Datum.

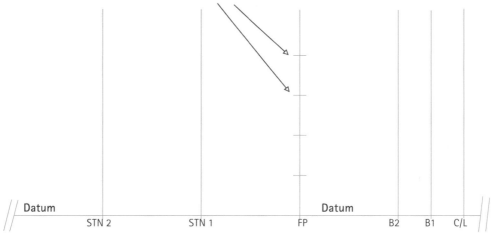

Step 7

The correct use of the tick stick (or lifting batten) is crucial in creating an accurate lofting of the boat.

1   Lay the tick stick along the line where the information to be transferred is located, in this case the FP.

2   Using a pencil or pen, pick up the marks set down in Step 6 onto the tick stick and transfer, in this case, to all of the remaining Stations, as well as the AP in the Profile View and the C/L and Buttocks in the Body Plan.

Note that by using a tick stick, any position is only 'measured' once. If it needs to be transferred, then using a tick stick guarantees consistency, because it eliminates the risk of any measuring errors that could occur if the same pieces of information were 'measured' several times.

Step 8

Using the Datum as a reference, transfer all of the marks (picked up in Step 7) onto all of the Stations etc, as shown in the drawing below. We can now draw in the Waterlines.

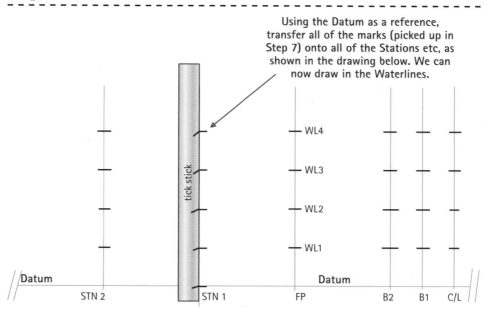

Step 9

Using the straight edge, join all the marks together to create the Waterlines. To prevent the line being 'staggered', always overlap the straight edge, as shown below.

Repeat this process for all of the other Waterlines.

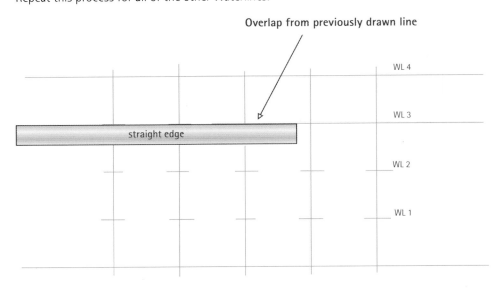

Step 10

With all of the Waterlines in place, the Lofting Grid will look similar to this. We can now look at drawing the grid for the Half-breadth (or Waterline) View.

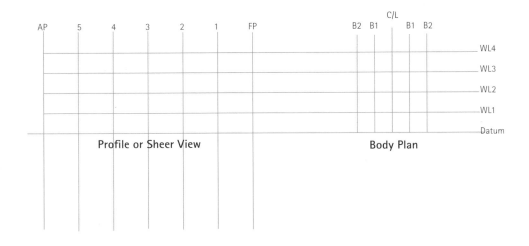

Step 11

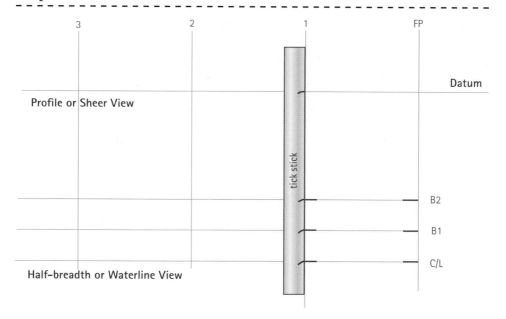

The Half-breadth View is typically drawn underneath the Profile View, with the Waterlines drawn out from the C/L 'towards' the Profile View (see page 5). The distance from the Datum to the C/L needs to be at least as great as the maximum half beam of the boat.

1   At the FP, measure down from the Datum and mark on the C/L and the Buttock Lines.

2   Using a tick stick, transfer these distances to all the other Stations.

3   Join these points together with a straight edge, using the same technique that we used to draw in the Waterlines in the Profile View: this ensures that our C/L is parallel to the Datum.

Step 12

The basic Lofting Grid is now finished and we're ready to start lofting our boat!

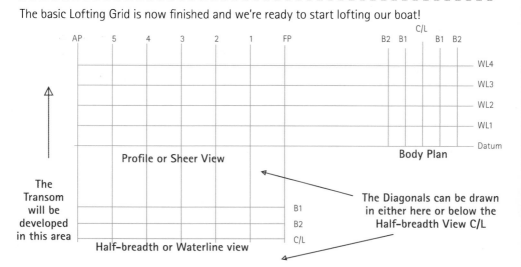

The Transom will be developed in this area

PLOTTING THE SHEER, PROFILE AND RABBETLINES IN THE PROFILE VIEW

PLOTTING THE SHEERLINE IN THE PROFILE VIEW

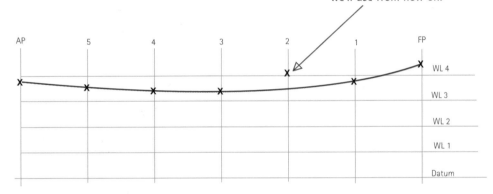

If using this offset gives us an unfair line, ignore the offset to achieve a fair line. The fair line measurement is what we'll use from now on.

From the Offset Table, find the Sheer heights of the FP, AP and Stations and plot them in their correct positions, using the Datum as a reference. With all of the points plotted, join them together with a batten. As we use a measurement from the Offset Table, put a line through it. This shows which offsets have been used, as they should only be used once. It's fine to adjust or ignore an offset measurement in order to get a fair line; just remember that from now on we'll use the 'fair line' measurement, and not the original offset.

PLOTTING THE PROFILE LINE IN THE PROFILE VIEW

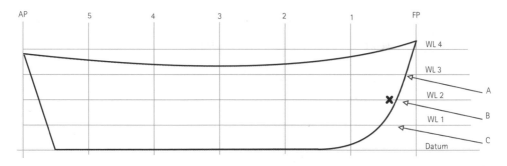

The Profile Line is plotted using a combination of the Profile heights at the Stations, taken from the Offset Table, and measurements taken 'along' the Waterline, points A, B and C etc, either from the FP measuring aft or from the AP measuring forward. This information will be found in either the Offset Table or as additional information on the Lines Drawing. (Time spent studying the Lines Drawing and Offset Table is rarely wasted.) As with plotting the Sheerline, if a measurement (such as at B) would give us an unfair line, then ignore it in favour of the fair line.

Next we'll look in greater detail at the process to plot first the forward and then the aft sections of the Profile Line in the Profile View.

PLOTTING THE PROFILE LINE IN THE PROFILE VIEW (FORWARD SECTION)

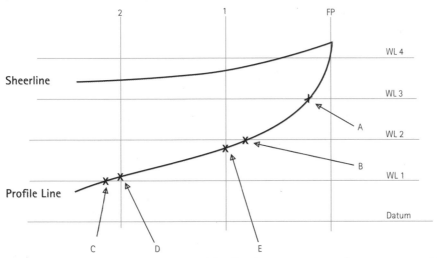

On a boat with a more complex forward Profile, the accurate use of measurements from both the Offset Table *and* the Lines Drawing is crucial in achieving a fair shape. As we can see from this drawing, the shape would be unobtainable without both sets of information. Points A, B and C are measured *along* the Waterlines, and points D and E are measured, in this case, upwards from a Datum Line.

PLOTTING THE PROFILE LINE IN THE PROFILE VIEW (AFT SECTION)

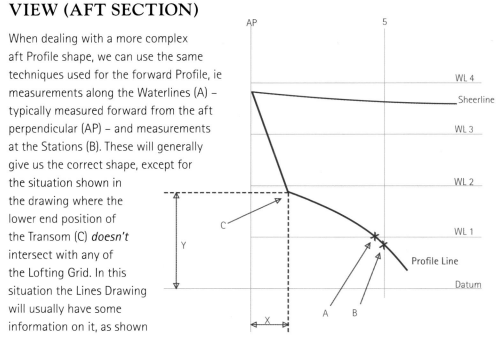

When dealing with a more complex aft Profile shape, we can use the same techniques used for the forward Profile, ie measurements along the Waterlines (A) – typically measured forward from the aft perpendicular (AP) – and measurements at the Stations (B). These will generally give us the correct shape, except for the situation shown in the drawing where the lower end position of the Transom (C) *doesn't* intersect with any of the Lofting Grid. In this situation the Lines Drawing will usually have some information on it, as shown on the right, to indicate where the base of the Transom ends. In this example, these co-ordinate 'lengths' have just been marked as X and Y.

With all of the information obtainable from the Lines Drawing and Offset Table, we should be able to draw in a fair Profile Line, however complex its shape is.

PLOTTING THE RABBETLINE IN THE PROFILE VIEW

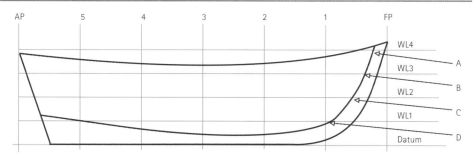

The Rabbetline is plotted in a similar way to the Profile Line, using a combination of the Rabbetline heights at the Stations (taken from the Offset Table) and measurements taken 'along' the Waterline, points A, B and C etc. The Rabbetline measurements may be either a measurement from the FP or a distance measured relative to the Profile Line – it depends entirely on the designer's preference.

Next we'll look in greater detail at the process to plot first the forward and then the aft sections of the Rabbetline in the Profile View. When these three lines (Sheer, Profile and Rabbet) have been plotted and faired, we can then move on to plot the Rabbetline and the Sheerline in the Half-breadth View.

PLOTTING THE RABBETLINE IN THE PROFILE VIEW
(FORWARD SECTION)

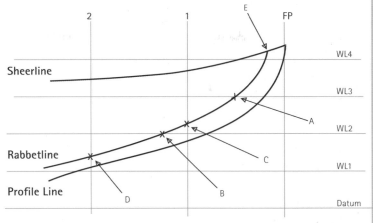

This point is usually measured out horizontally from the FP

The Rabbetline is plotted using a similar process used to plot the Profile Line. Points A and B are measured along the Waterline, but remember, they can be referenced either from the FP or from the Profile Line, depending on the design you are lofting. Similarly, points C and D are measured vertically on the Stations but they can be referenced either from the Datum or from the Profile Line – again, it depends on the design.

The other point to plot is the intersection of the Rabbetline with the Sheerline (E). This is relatively close to the FP and would typically be measured out horizontally using a set square or builder's square.

PLOTTING THE RABBETLINE IN THE PROFILE VIEW
(AFT SECTION)

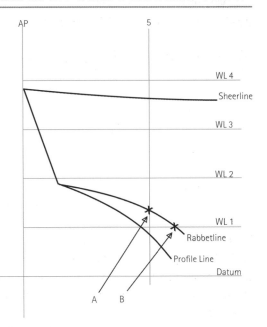

The Rabbetline in the aft section can be plotted using a similar set of techniques used to plot the Profile Line.

Measurement (A) will be plotted vertically on the Station. As with the forward section of the Rabbetline, this measurement will be referenced either from the Datum or from the existing Profile Line. Measurement (B) will be plotted horizontally along the Waterline and, as with the forward section, will be referenced off either the AP or the existing Profile Line. As with the forward section, the points of reference depend on the designer of the boat; all we need to do is interpret the information in front of us.

The Rabbetline has ended at the same intersection point as the Profile Line. If there is any variation in this, the end point can be plotted using the same co-ordinate process used for the Transom/Profile Line intersection point.

PLOTTING THE RABBET AND SHEERLINES IN THE HALF-BREADTH/ WATERLINE VIEW

PLOTTING THE RABBETLINE IN THE HALF-BREADTH/WATERLINE VIEW

Step 1 (of 5)

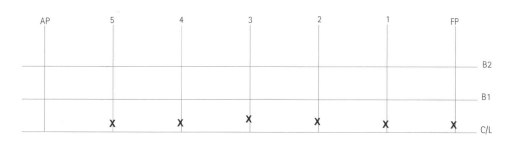

The Rabbetline is plotted using measurements (Half-breadths) taken from the Offset Table. The positions are plotted at the FP and Stations as a distance measured out from the C/L. The Rabbetline doesn't end at the AP – unless the boat has a plumb Transom – its end position is picked up from the Profile View and transferred to the Half-breadth View. The techniques used to do this are shown over the following pages.

Step 2

1. Lay the tick stick down as shown in the drawing, using a roofing or set square to ensure that it's parallel to the Waterlines.

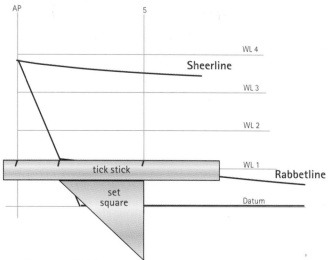

2. Mark on/pick up the distance from the AP or Stn 5 to the intersection point of the Rabbetline with the Transom.

3. Transfer this distance to the Half-breadth View.

Step 3

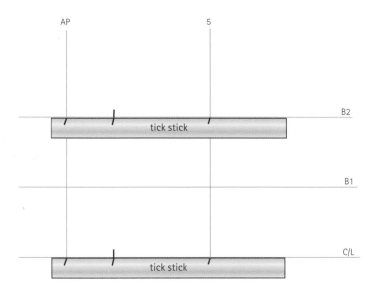

1. Lay the tick stick on the C/L, using the same reference point as in Step 2, and mark on the Rabbetline/Transom intersection point picked up in Step 2.

2. Repeat this process at either B1 or B2.

3. Step 4 will show you how to use these points to plot the true Rabbetline/Transom intersection position in the Half-breadth View.

Step 4

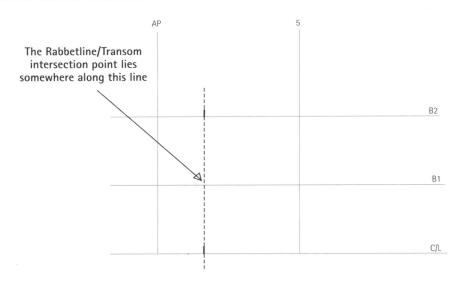

1   Using a straight edge, join together the two points plotted in Step 3.

2   The true intersection point of the Rabbetline/Transom lies somewhere along this line.

3   The Rabbetline Half-breadth at the Transom can be found in the Offset Table – all we have to do now is plot it along this line exactly as we did with all of the other Rabbetline Half-breadths.

4   We now have all of the information needed to plot the Rabbetline in the Half-breadth View.

Step 5

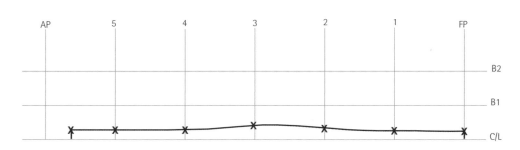

With the points plotted, all that remains is to join them together with a batten, which will then give us the shape of the Rabbetline in the Half-breadth View. Typically, the end positions will then just be squared back to the C/L. Any 'flare' in the Rabbetline, in this case between Stns 1 and 4, will be due to the Keel's Waterline shape, but every boat will be different.

     With the Rabbetline plotted, we can now look at plotting the Sheerline in the Half-breadth View.

PLOTTING THE SHEERLINE IN THE HALF-BREADTH/WATERLINE VIEW

Step 1 (of 5)

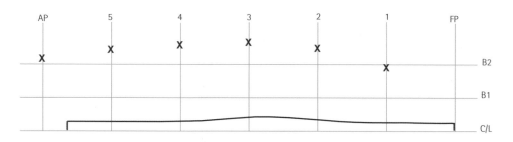

As with the Rabbetline, the Sheerline is plotted using measurements (Half-breadths) taken from the Offset Table. As before, these positions are plotted as a distance measured out from the C/L. The main difference is how we find the intersection point for the Sheer and Rabbetline. For this we will again use a tick stick to find the distance aft of the FP that the Sheerline and the Rabbetline intersect in the Profile View (see Step 2). This measurement is then plotted along the Rabbetline in the Half-breadth View, giving the true Sheerline/Rabbetline intersection point. This technique is shown on the following pages.

Step 2

1 Lay the tick stick down as shown in the drawing, using a roofing or set square to ensure that it is parallel to the Waterline.

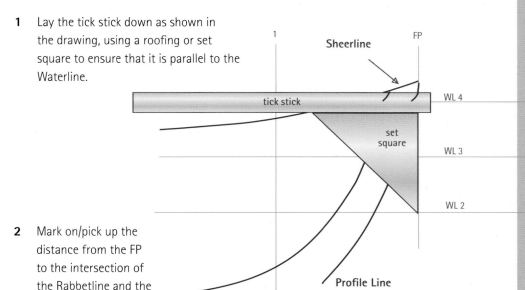

2 Mark on/pick up the distance from the FP to the intersection of the Rabbetline and the Sheerline.

3 Transfer this distance to the Half-breadth View.

Step 3

1 Using the FP as a reference, lay the tick stick on the C/L and plot the Rabbetline/ Sheerline intersection point picked up in Step 2.

2 Repeat this process on either B1 or B2.

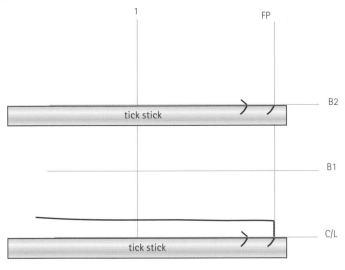

In Step 4, we'll see how these points allow us to find the true intersection point of the Sheerline with the Rabbetline.

Step 4

1 Using a straight edge, join together the two points, plotted in Step 3, with a faint line.

2 Where this faint line intersects the Rabbetline is the true end position of the Sheerline in the Half-breadth View.

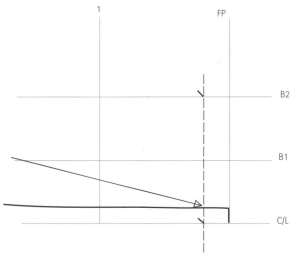

We now have all the information needed to plot the Sheerline in the Half-breadth View.

Step 5

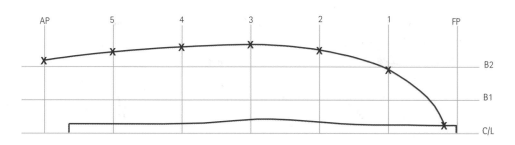

With all of the points plotted, we can now join them together using a batten, held in position using either nails or lofting/spline weights. Remember, as with the Sheerline in the Profile View – or, in fact, any of the lines drawn so far – the important thing is to achieve a fair line, even if that means we have to miss out one or more of the points.

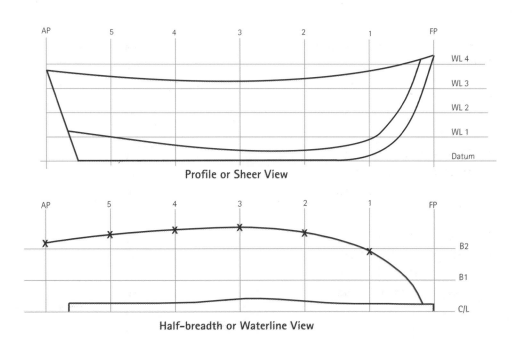

Profile or Sheer View

Half-breadth or Waterline View

The five basic lines for the shape of the boat are now complete. These are fixed, but any or all of the other points and lines we're going to plot can be corrected if required, to achieve a fair line. We'll now move on and plot all of the Stations in the Body Plan.

PLOTTING THE STATION LINES IN THE BODY PLAN

Step 1 (of 11)

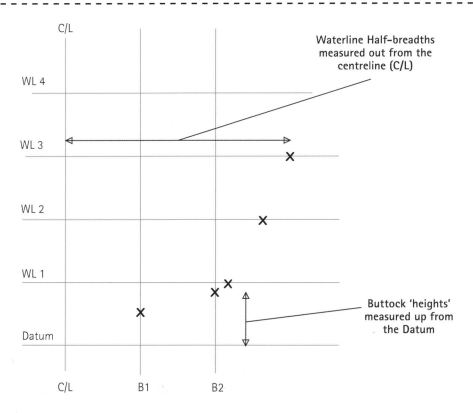

For each Station (and the Transom) that we're about to draw, we get its shape using information from the Offset Table *and* any existing information we already have. Depending on the design we're lofting, the Station Lines can be lofted using either a combination of Waterline Half-breadths and Buttock heights, shown in the drawing above, or this information *plus* the addition of a Diagonal measurement for each Station (see alternative Step 1 shown on the opposite page).

The Offset Table gives us:

1   Waterline Half-breadths (for each Station) measured out from the C/L

2   Buttock 'heights' for each Station (where the Station crosses a Buttock Line). It is easy to miss out these points and use only the Waterline Half-breadths, but the Buttock heights are needed to create the true shape of each Station.

Alternative Step 1

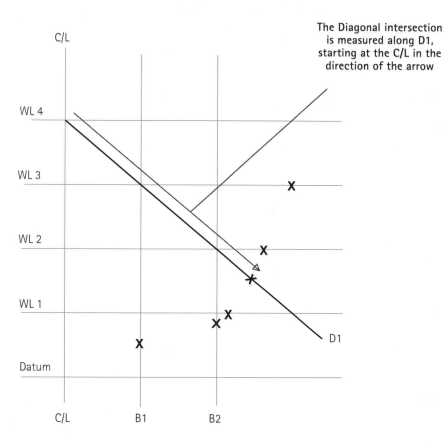

The Diagonal intersection is measured along D1, starting at the C/L in the direction of the arrow

If the Offset Table also has information for a Diagonal measurement, then we would use the same Waterline Half-breadths and Buttock heights used in the previous drawing *plus* the additional Diagonal information. As mentioned earlier, any Diagonals in the Offset Table need to be set out at the points specified by the designer for them to work correctly. In this case, the Diagonal starts on the C/L at WL 4 and intersects at WL 2 and B2, as shown in the drawing. Any Diagonal offset measurement is then taken along this line starting at the C/L, as shown in the drawing. If a boat design has Diagonal offsets there will probably be at least two or three, giving a range of extra information for plotting the Stations in the Body Plan. However, in order to complete each Station in the Body Plan we need to plot the Station intersections with the Rabbet, Profile and Sheerlines, and the following pages will show you how to do this.

FINDING AND PLOTTING THE STATION INTERSECTION WITH THE RABBETLINE AND PROFILE LINE (USING STN 1 AS A WORKED EXAMPLE)

Step 2

In the Profile View, lay the tick stick along Stn 1, using the Datum as a reference, and pick up the Profile Line and the Rabbetline.

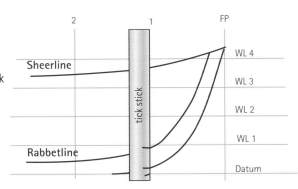

In the Half-breadth View, lay the tick stick along Stn 1, using the C/L as a reference, and pick up the Rabbetline. In this case, the base of the Keel (the Profile) is the same Half-breadth as the Rabbetline.

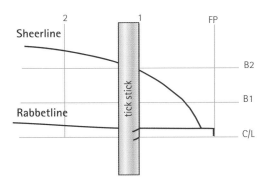

Step 3

1   Place the tick stick vertically along the C/L, using the Datum as a reference, and transfer the marks picked up from the Profile View onto the Body Plan C/L.

2   Repeat this process using either B1 or B2.

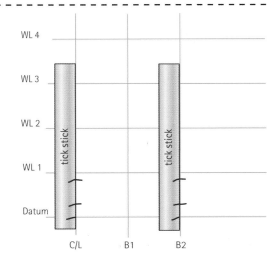

Step 4

1   Using a straight edge or
    ruler, join together the points
    marked on the C/L and Buttock
    Line with a faint line.

2   The true end positions of the
    Rabbetline and the base of
    the Keel lie somewhere along
    these horizontal lines.

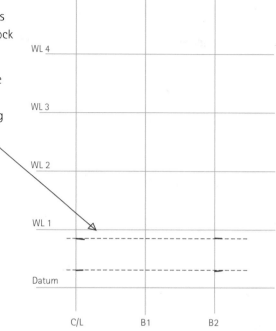

The next drawing will show how we transfer the Half-breadth information, picked up from Step 2, onto the Body Plan.

Step 5

Using the C/L as a reference, lay
the tick stick along these dashed
lines and transfer the Half-breadth
information for the Rabbetline
and Profile Line (picked up in Step
2). These points are the true end
positions of the Rabbetline and the
base of the Keel/Profile.

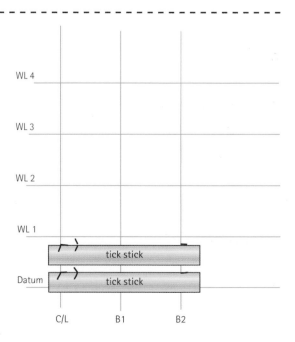

Step 6

We now have the true end position of Stn 1. As mentioned earlier, the faired line *must* intersect with the Rabbetline position, even if we ignore one or more of the other points in order to achieve a fair line.

We'll now use a similar process to plot the true position of the Sheerline in the Body Plan.

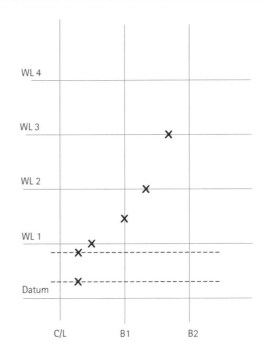

Step 7

1 In the Profile View, lay the tick stick along Stn 1 and pick up the Sheerline height, using either the Datum or any of the Waterlines as a reference mark.

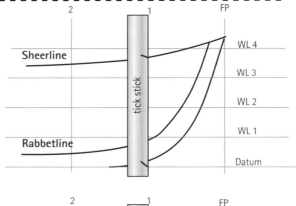

2 In the Half-breadth View, lay the tick stick along Stn 1, using the C/L as a reference, and pick up the Sheerline Half-breadth.

3 Transfer this information to the Body Plan.

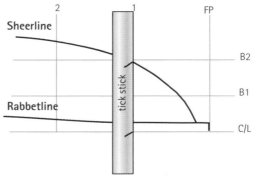

Step 8

1 Place the tick stick vertically along the C/L, using the Datum as a reference, and transfer the marks picked up from the Profile View onto the Body Plan.

2 Move the tick stick over to B2 and repeat the process.

We're using B2 because the Sheer intersection point is much further out from the C/L than the Rabbetline intersection point. By doing this we ensure that the line we're about to draw is truly horizontal and parallel to the Datum.

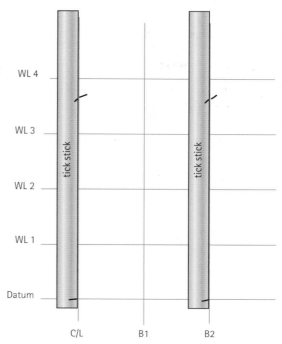

Step 9

Using a straight edge or ruler, join together the points marked on the C/L and Buttock Line. The true end position of the Sheerline lies somewhere along this horizontal line. The next drawing will show how we transfer the Half-breadth information, picked up from Step 7, onto the Body Plan.

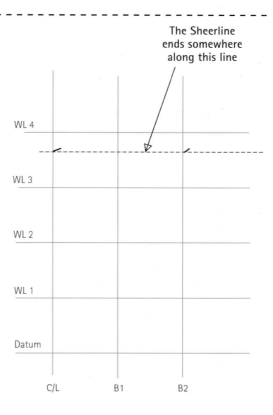

33

Step 10

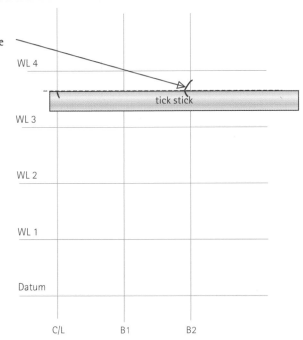

This is the true end position of the Sheerline at Stn 1

tick stick

WL 4

WL 3

WL 2

WL 1

Datum

C/L   B1   B2

Lay the tick stick along this line, using the C/L as a reference, and transfer the Sheerline Half-breadth information picked up in Step 7. This point gives us the true end position of the Sheerline at Stn 1.

We now have all the information needed to plot Stn 1 in the Body Plan.

Step 11

It's important to note that the points at the Sheer and the Rabbetline are fixed (from previously faired lines) and cannot be adjusted. All of the other points are potentially inaccurate – due to drafting or measuring errors – and are only a guide. Therefore, when fairing the curve with a batten the most important thing at this stage is to end up with a fair line (by eye) that passes through the majority of the points. At this stage we don't actually know which points are correct and which are not, but later on we'll correct any differences when we plot and fair the Buttocks and then the Diagonals.

Now repeat this whole process (Steps 1 to 11) for all of the remaining Stations and the Transom. We should then have a drawing that looks similar to the one on the opposite page.

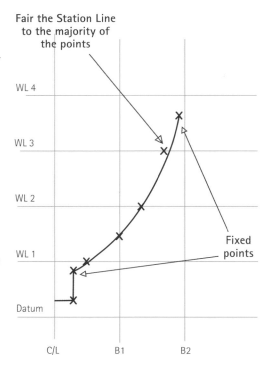

Fair the Station Line to the majority of the points

Fixed points

WL 4

WL 3

WL 2

WL 1

Datum

C/L   B1   B2

34

The Body Plan should now look something similar to this, depending on the boat that you are lofting. We can now use the Body Plan and information from the Sheer/Profile View to draw all of the Waterlines in the Half-breadth View.

With all of the lines drawn in the Body Plan, it's tempting to just draw in a curved shape for the top surface of the Transom. The technique for plotting the true shape of the Transom is shown later on.

Join the Sheer points together if you want to, but you don't have to, as the Sheerline in the Body Plan gives us a 'compressed' perspective. This means that the line cannot really be used to collect information from it.

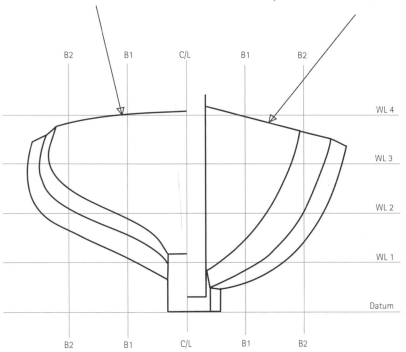

Note: At this point, all of the information from the Offset Table should have been used. From now on, any information needed to complete the lofting will come from our own drawing!

PLOTTING THE WATERLINES IN THE HALF-BREADTH VIEW

Step 1 (of 11)

The Waterlines can be drawn in any order, but for this worked example we'll use WL 2.

1   Lay the tick stick along WL 2 and pick up, in this case, the following intersection points: C/L, Stns 1, 2, 3, 4 and 5 and the Transom.

2   Transfer this information to the Half-breadth View.

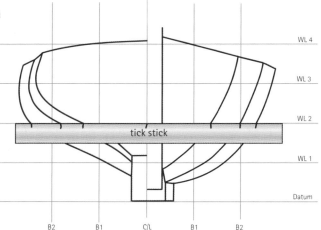

Remember to pick up the actual faired intersection line and *not* the offset measurement (if indeed there was any difference).

Alternative Step 1

Using a tick stick long enough to span the whole width of the Body Plan can be both awkward and impractical. It's generally easier to use a shorter tick stick that only needs to be long enough to cover the maximum Half-breadth of the Body Plan.

   As you can see from the drawing, the tick stick is laid to pick up one side of

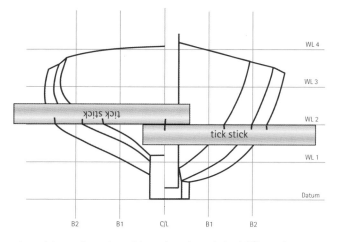

the Body Plan and is then rotated to pick up the other side, using the original C/L mark as a common reference point. This is the method that will be used from this point.

Step 2

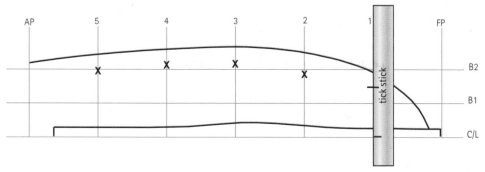

1   Lay the tick stick on Stn 1, using the C/L as a reference, and then transfer the Half-breadth of WL 2 (picked up in Step 1) onto the Half-breadth View.

2   Repeat this procedure for all of the remaining Stations from WL 2, in this case Stns 2, 3, 4 and 5.

If the Transom of the boat is not raked we can also plot the Transom Half-breadth on the AP. However, this boat, like many others, has a raked/angled Transom and the Waterline will end somewhere forward of the AP. The following steps (3, 4, 5 and 6) will show you how to plot the Transom end position of the Waterline.

Step 3

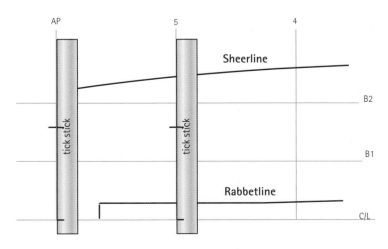

As mentioned earlier, because the Transom is raked/angled, we can't just end the Transom on the AP. We can, however, draw in a line where we know the Waterline intersects the Transom.

1   As shown on the drawing above, lay the tick stick along the AP, using the C/L as a reference, and plot the Transom Half-breadth for WL 2, using information picked up from the Body Plan in Step 1.

2   Repeat this process on the next Station, in this case Stn 5.

Step 4

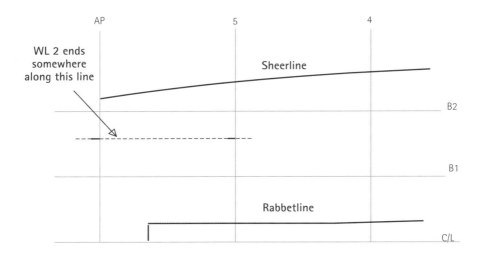

1   Using a straight edge or ruler, join these two points together with a faint pencil line.

2   The actual Transom intersection for WL 2 lies somewhere along this line. To get the actual distance along the line, we'll need to look at WL 2 in the Sheer/Profile View.

Step 5

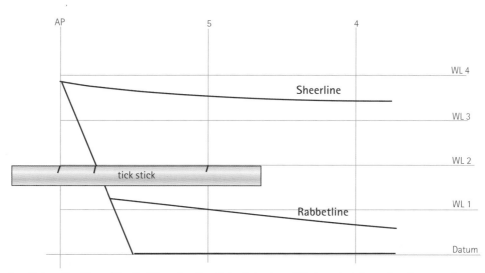

1   Using the Sheer/Profile View, lay the tick stick along WL 2 and pick up the distance from either the AP to the Transom intersection or the distance from Stn 5 to the Transom intersection.

2   Transfer this to the Half-breadth View to plot the intersection point of WL 2 with the Transom.

Step 6

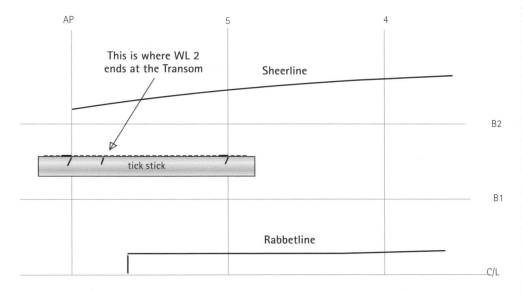

1   Lay the tick stick with the information picked up from Step 5 along the line drawn in Step 4.

2   Align the tick stick with either the AP or Stn 5 – whichever one was used in Step 5 to pick up the information – and plot the Transom intersection point onto the line.

Step 7

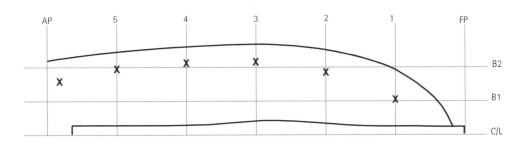

We now have all of the information needed to plot WL 2 in the Half-breadth View, except for the intersection point of WL 2 with the Rabbetline. The technique needed to find this point is similar to that used to find the Transom intersection point, but we need to use the forward section of the Sheer/Profile View. Steps 8, 9 and 10 will show you how to find this point.

Step 8

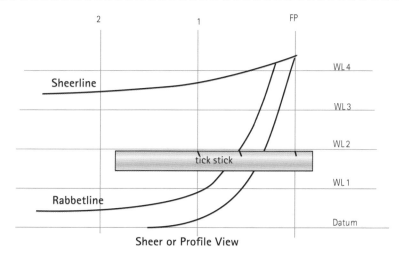

Sheer or Profile View

1   Lay the tick stick along WL 2 and pick up the distance from either the FP to the Rabbetline intersection or the distance from Stn 1 to the Rabbetline intersection.

2   Transfer this information to the Half-breadth View and plot the intersection point of WL 2 with the Rabbetline.

Step 9

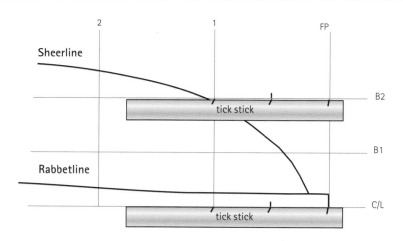

1   In the Half-breadth View, lay the tick stick along the C/L, using either the FP or Stn 1 as a reference, and transfer the Rabbetline intersection distance (picked up in Step 8) along this line.

2   Repeat this process, using either B1 or B2.

Step 10

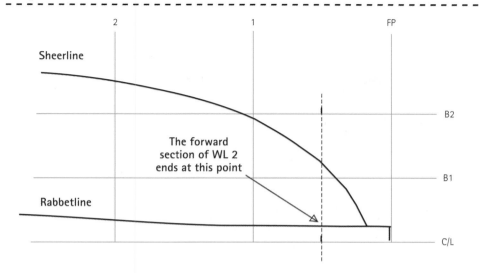

Using a straight edge, join these two points together with a faint line. Where this line crosses the Rabbetline is the forward intersection point of WL 2 in the Half-breadth View. With this point plotted, we now have all the information needed to draw WL 2 in the Half-breadth View.

Step 11

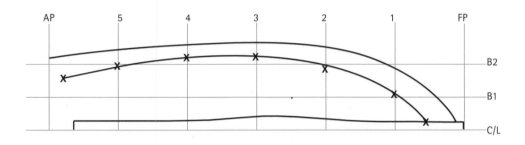

Using a batten, draw a line going through the points that have been plotted, but as with the Body Plan, achieving a 'fair line' is more important than simply 'joining all the points together' – as you can see in WL 2, to get a 'fair line' we have ignored the points at Stns 2 and 5. Remember, the only definite fixed points are where the Waterline intersects with the Rabbetline and the Transom. Any discrepancies between the Half-breadth View and the Body Plan will be initially resolved when we plot the Buttock Lines, and any final differences will be resolved when we plot the Diagonals.

Now repeat the process (Steps 1 to 11) and plot all of the remaining Waterlines in the Half-breadth View. We should now have a drawing that looks similar to the one on the following page.

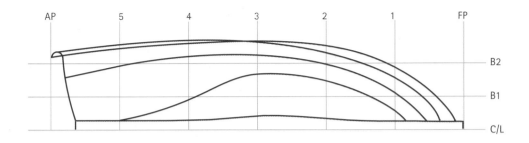

When all of the Waterlines have been drawn in the Half-breadth View, we can join all the Transom points together to show the shape of the Transom in the Half-breadth View. But please be aware that the shape we see is not a true representation of the Transom because of the angle at which we are looking at it... But more about that later when we come to develop and expand the Transom to show its true size and shape.

With all of the Waterlines plotted and faired, we're now ready to plot the Buttock Lines in the Profile View, using information picked up from our Body Plan and Half-breadth Views.

PLOTTING THE BUTTOCK LINES IN THE PROFILE VIEW

In order to plot the Buttock Lines in the Profile View, we're going to use information from lines we have already drawn in both the Body Plan and the Half-breadth Views, and combine them together to plot and draw the Buttock Lines in the Profile View. The process we'll use to do this is shown below.

1   Pick up the Buttock/Station Line intersection points from the Body Plan and transfer them to the Profile View, where they will be plotted vertically on their respective Stations.

2   Plot the Buttock/Transom intersection point, using information picked up from the Body Plan.

3   Pick up the Buttock/Waterline intersection points from the Half-breadth View and transfer them to the Profile View, where they will be plotted horizontally along their respective Waterlines.

4   Plot the Buttock/Sheer intersection point using information picked up from the Half-breadth View.

Step 1 (of 12)

1   Lay the tick stick on B1, forward section, using either the Datum or any Waterline as a reference. Mark on the Buttock intersections of Stns 1, 2 and 3. Don't use the Body Plan to find the Sheer intersection point as it is not an accurate line, due to the foreshortening effect referred to earlier.

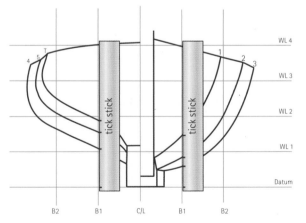

2   Repeat this process for the aft section, picking up the Buttock intersections of Stns 4 and 5 and the Transom (T).

3   Transfer these Buttock intersection points to the Profile View.

43

Step 2

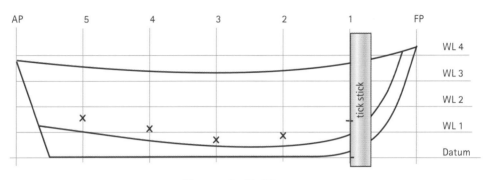

Sheer or Profile View

1 Starting at Stn 1, place the tick stick on the Datum Line (or your reference Waterline) and plot the height of Buttock 1 on Stn 1.

2 Repeat this process for all of the remaining Stations – but *not* for the Transom.

3 To find the Buttock/Transom intersection, see Steps 3 and 4.

Step 3

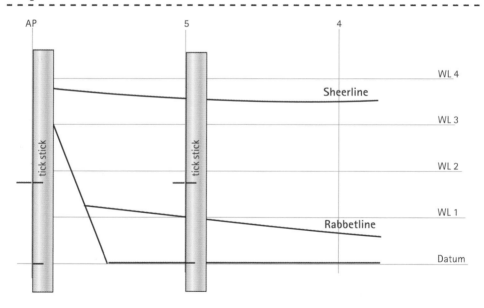

As the Transom is angled/raked, we can't plot the end position of the Buttock Line with the same method we used for the Stations. Instead, we'll use the following technique:

1 Lay the tick stick on the AP, using the Datum (or your Waterline) as a reference, and plot the height of B1.

2 Repeat this process at Stn 5.

Step 4

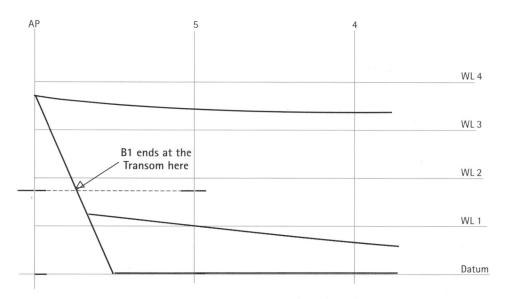

1   Using a straight edge, join together these two points with a feint line.

2   The point at which this line crosses the Transom is the correct end position of B1 in the Profile View.

Step 5

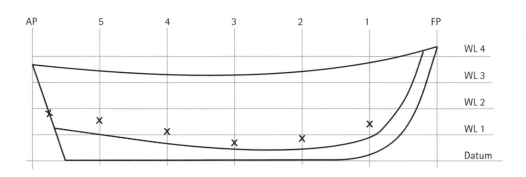

We now have the Buttock heights, picked up from the Body Plan, plotted in the Profile View. Next we need to pick up the Buttock/Waterline and Sheer intersection points from the Half-breadth View and plot them in the Profile View. This will then give us a complete set of points with which to plot the Buttock Line. The techniques to do this are shown in Steps 6 to 11.

Step 6

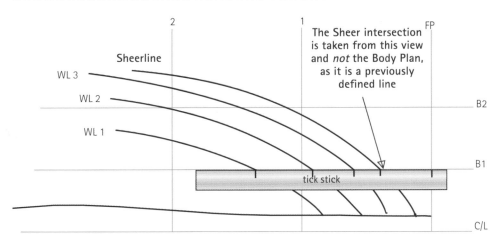

We're now going to pick up the Buttock intersection 'lengths' in the Half-breadth View and transfer them to the Profile View. Because of the size of boats in general, we'll deal with the 'forward' section first and the 'aft' section separately, although the techniques used are basically the same.

1   Lay the tick stick along B1, using the FP as a reference, and pick up the intersection points of B1 with the Sheer and all of the Waterlines that it crosses.

2   Transfer these points to the Profile View and plot them along their respective Waterlines.

Step 7

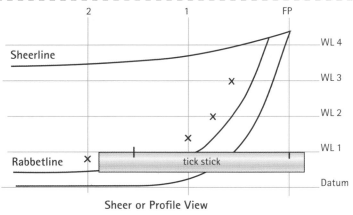

Sheer or Profile View

We can now plot the Buttock/Waterline intersection points, picked up in Step 6, onto the Profile View.

1   Lay the tick stick along WL 1, using the FP as a reference, and plot the Waterline intersection 'length', picked up in the Half-breadth View, onto the Profile View.

2   Repeat this process for all of the remaining Waterlines but *not* the Sheer intersection point. Steps 8 and 9 will show you how to plot the Buttock/Sheer intersection point.

Step 8

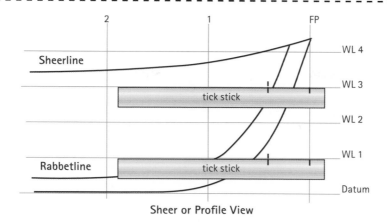

Sheer or Profile View

We can now plot the Sheer intersection point of the Buttock Line.

1   Using the FP as a reference, lay the tick stick along any Waterline and plot the Sheer intersection point, picked up in Step 6, onto that Waterline.

2   Repeat this process using any other Waterline – preferably as widely spaced as possible to give a more accurate line. Step 9 will show you how to use these points to plot the true Buttock/Sheer intersection point.

Step 9

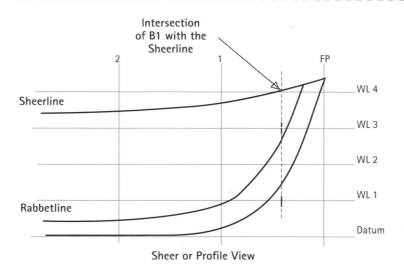

Sheer or Profile View

Using a straight edge, join together the two points plotted in Step 8. Draw a faint line through these two points and extend the line until it crosses the Sheerline. This is the true Sheer intersection point of the Buttock Line. We now have all of the information needed to draw the forward section of the Buttock Line.

Step 10

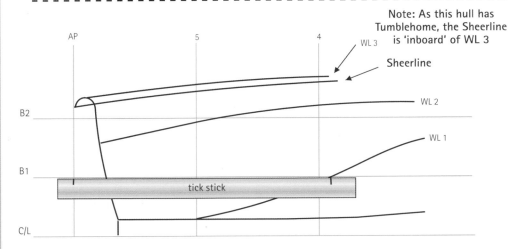

Note: As this hull has Tumblehome, the Sheerline is 'inboard' of WL 3

We're now going to pick up the Buttock/Waterline intersection 'lengths' from the aft section of the Half-breadth View and transfer them to the Profile View, using basically the same techniques we used for the forward section.

1   Lay the tick stick along B1, using the AP as a reference, and pick up the intersection points of B1 with all of the Waterlines that it crosses (in this case, there is only WL 1 that crosses B1). Don't pick up the Transom intersection because it's already been plotted in Steps 3 and 4 and the Transom in this view is not a true shape.

2   Transfer these points to the Profile View and plot them along their respective Waterlines.

Step 11

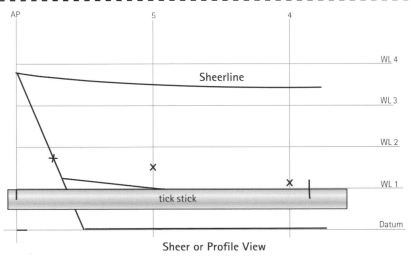

Sheer or Profile View

1   Lay the tick stick along WL 1, using the AP as a reference, and plot the Waterline 'length', picked up in Step 10 from the Half-breadth View, onto the Profile View.

2   Repeat this process for any other Waterlines that the Buttock Line has crossed.

Step 12

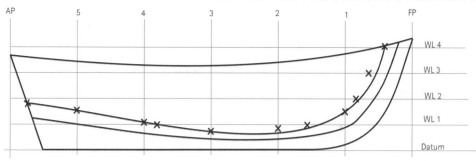

Sheer or Profile View

We now have all the information needed to plot B1 in the Profile View. Please note that apart from the 'fixed points' at the Sheer and Transom, none of the points are fixed; the aim is to achieve a fair line that runs through the majority of the points we've plotted.

Remember that as there were almost certainly discrepancies in both the Body Plan and the Half-breadth View – eg the 'fair line' did not go through all of the offset measurements – it is almost certain that to get a fair Buttock Line we'll have to ignore some of the points we have just plotted, either on the Station Line or Waterline or both. Don't worry if you have to do this – they'll get corrected later on.

Now repeat this process (Steps 1 to 12) and plot all of the remaining Buttock Lines *before* you start correcting any discrepancies – to see if any 'error patterns' emerge.

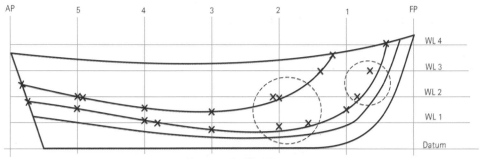

Sheer or Profile View

With all of the Buttocks plotted, our drawing will look something like the one shown above, but obviously every boat will be different. As mentioned earlier, we may see an 'error pattern' emerge in the Buttocks – ie the errors or differences may be similar for all of the Buttocks that have been drawn. As you can see in the drawing, some of the errors in B2 are similar to the errors in B1.

It's apparent from this drawing that there are two main areas where the fair line of the Buttocks means we have to ignore some of the points picked up from the Body Plan and the Half-breadth View. For clarity, these two areas have been circled: there's an error pattern where both of the Buttocks intersect with Stn 2 and their related Waterlines, and there's also the area on Buttock 1 as it approaches the Sheerline.

Before we go on to correct the Buttocks in the Body Plan and the Profile View, we are going to look at the techniques used to plot a Buttock Line that *does not* end at the Transom.

Example of a 're-curve' Buttock Line

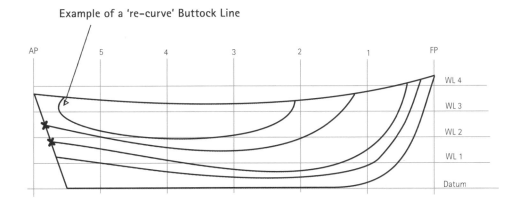

If the boat we're lofting has a Buttock Line which doesn't end at the Transom, we can't find its finish position using Steps 3 and 4. In addition, the boat may have some 'Tumblehome' (a situation where the Sheer is not the widest point at any given Station). In this situation, the Buttock Line will have a 're-curve' shape, ie it comes back on itself. Don't worry, however, as this is what's meant to happen.

In the drawing above, there's a 're-curve' Buttock Line drawn in, simply to illustrate its shape. The following pages will show you how to pick up the extra information needed to draw in a Buttock Line like this.

PLOTTING THE BUTTOCK LINES IN THE PROFILE VIEW IF A BUTTOCK LINE *DOESN'T* END AT THE TRANSOM

Step 1 (of 7)

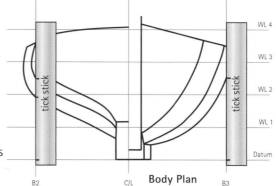

1   Lay the tick stick on B3 (forward section), using the Datum as a reference, and mark on the Buttock intersections of the Stations.

2   Repeat this process for the aft section, picking up the Buttock intersections of the Stations but *not* the Transom, as B3 doesn't pass through the Transom.

3   Transfer these Buttock intersection heights to the Profile View, using the same technique used before with the other Buttock Lines.

4   The technique used to find and plot the aft Buttock/Sheer intersection point is shown in the following pages.

Step 2

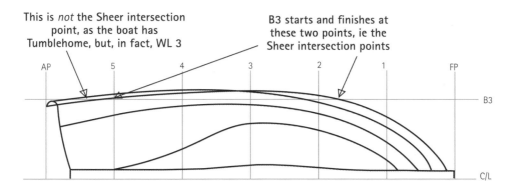

As we can see from the drawing above, B3 doesn't pass through the Transom, and therefore the Buttock Line will start and finish along the Sheerline, at the two points shown above. Previously, we saw how to pick up, transfer and plot the forward Buttock/Sheer intersection point. Basically, we just need to follow the same process for the aft Buttock/Sheer intersection, except we'll use the AP, not FP, as a reference (see Step 3). The end result will be a Buttock Line similar in shape to the one in the previous Profile View drawing.
Please note: B3 is only drawn in for illustrative purposes.

Step 3

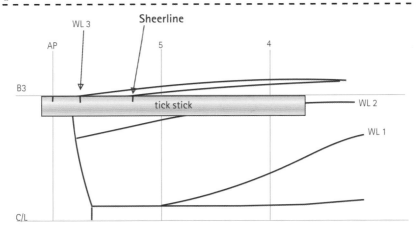

1   Lay the tick stick along B3, using the AP as a reference, and pick up the intersection points of B3 with all of the Waterlines and the Sheerline.

2   Transfer these points to the Profile View (see Step 4).

Remember, as this Buttock Line will be a 're-curve' shape, the Sheer intersection point is *not* the one closest to the AP.

Step 4

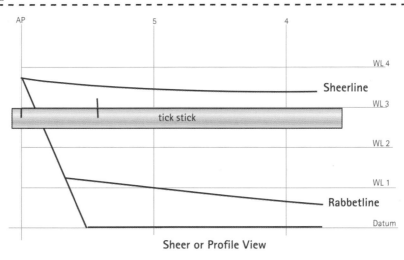

Sheer or Profile View

1   Lay the tick stick along WL 3, using the AP as a reference, and transfer the Waterline 'length', picked up from the Half-breadth View in Step 3, onto the Profile View.

2   Repeat this process for any other Waterlines that crossed B3.

We're now ready to plot the Sheer/Buttock intersection point.

Step 5

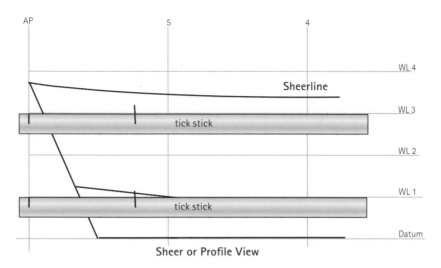

Sheer or Profile View

1   Using the AP as a reference, lay the tick stick along any Waterline, in this case WL 1, and plot the Sheer intersection point 'length' that we picked up in Step 3.

2   Repeat this process using any other Waterline, in this case WL 3. Step 6 will show you how to find the actual Buttock/Sheer intersection point.

Step 6

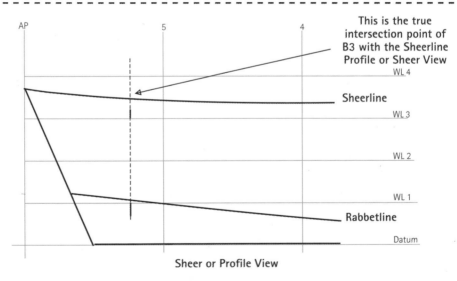

Sheer or Profile View

Using a straight edge, join together the two points plotted in Step 5. Draw a line through these points and extend the line until it crosses the Sheerline. This is the true intersection point of the Buttock Line.

We're now ready to finally plot the aft section of B3.

Step 7

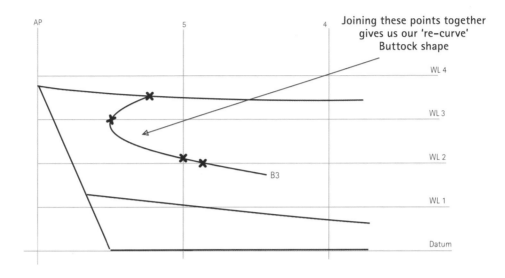

With all of the points plotted, we can now use a batten to join them together to draw in the aft section of B3. The forward section will have been plotted and drawn as normal with the techniques we used earlier.

With all of the Buttock Lines plotted and faired in the Profile/Sheer View, we can now fair/correct the Body Plan and the Half-breadth View so that they 'tie in' with the Profile View. The following pages will show the techniques needed to do this.

FAIRING THE BUTTOCK LINES IN THE PROFILE VIEW

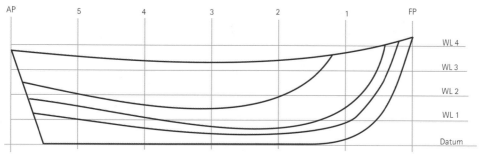

Sheer or Profile View

We can now start correcting the Station Lines in the Body Plan, and the Waterlines in the Half-breadth View, so that they tie in with the Buttock Lines. Some people may tell you to leave any corrections until the Diagonals have been plotted. The main problem with doing this is that the information for plotting the Diagonals would then be picked up from an 'uncorrected' Body Plan. If we happen to end up with a 'fair' Diagonal, it won't relate to any other line, and so how do we know which line to trust? Therefore, if we correct the Body Plan and the Half-breadth View *before* plotting the Diagonals, we can then trust any measurements used to plot the Diagonals and make any final corrections.

Step 1 (of 8)

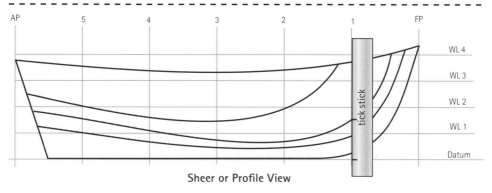

Sheer or Profile View

1   Lay the tick stick on Stn 1, using the Datum as a reference, and pick up the 'faired/corrected' Buttock height intersection points.

2   Repeat this process for all the other Stations.

Transfer this information to the Body Plan and 'correct' the Buttock/Station Line intersection points.

55

Step 2

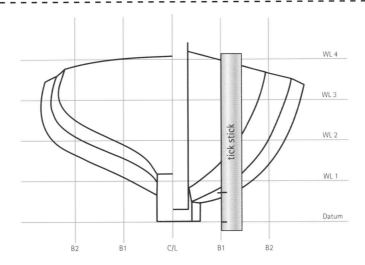

1   Lay the tick stick on B1, using the Datum as a reference, and plot the corrected Buttock intersection points, picked up in Step 1, onto the Stations.

2   Repeat this process for all of the other Buttock/Station corrections picked up from Step 1.

3   'Re-fair' the Stations using these corrected Buttock points.

4   We can then transfer these re-faired Waterline Half-breadths to the Half-breadth View.

Step 3

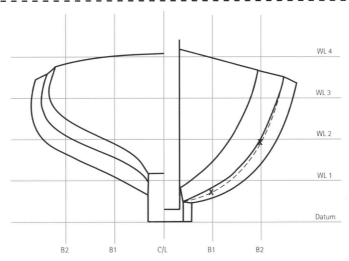

Having re-faired the Stations using the corrected Buttock points, this will almost certainly mean that there will now be discrepancies in the Waterline Half-breadths. (For clarity, the re-faired line has been drawn in as a broken line – to make it easier to see any difference.) Transfer these re-faired Waterline Half-breadths from the Body Plan to the Half-breadth View.

Step 4

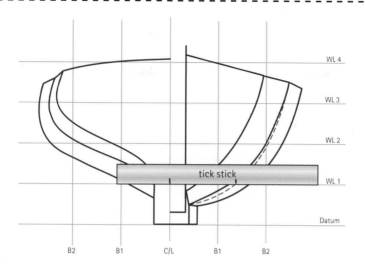

1 Lay the tick stick on WL 1, using the C/L as a reference, and pick up all of the re-faired Waterline Half-breadths.

2 Repeat this process for any of the other Waterlines where any corrections have been made.

3 Transfer these corrected Waterline Half-breadths from the Body Plan to the Half-breadth View.

Step 5

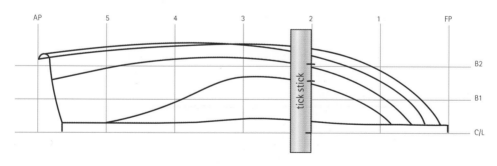

1 Using the C/L as a reference, lay the tick stick on any Station, in this case Stn 2, and transfer the 'corrected' Waterline Half-breadths, picked up from the Body Plan in Step 4, onto the Station.

2 Repeat this process for all the other Stations, but don't re-fair the Waterlines at this time, as we have to get some more information from the Profile View.

Step 6

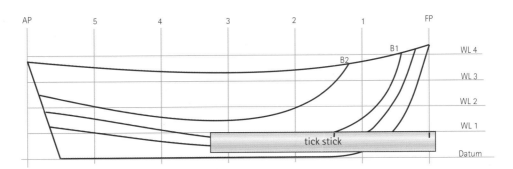

1   Lay the tick stick on WL 1, using the FP as a reference, and pick up the 'faired and corrected' Buttock/Waterline intersection points.

2   Repeat this process for the other Waterlines. If the boat is anything other than a very small dinghy or skiff, we'll probably need to pick up and transfer the forward and aft 'corrections' separately.

3   Transfer this information to the Half-breadth View and make any corrections required to the Buttock/Waterline intersection points.

Step 7

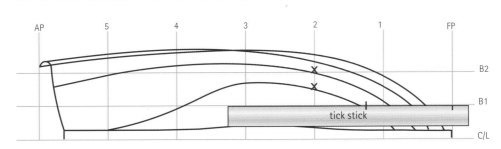

1   Lay the tick stick on B1, using the FP as a reference, and transfer the 'corrected' Waterline/Buttock intersection points picked up from the Profile View in Step 6 onto the Buttock Line.

2   Repeat this process for all of the other Buttocks where corrections need to be made. As with picking up this information (Step 6), we'll probably need to transfer the forward and aft sections separately, unless we're lofting a very small dinghy or skiff.

Step 8

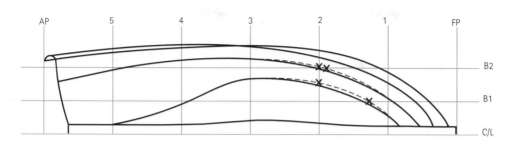

We now have a complete set of 'corrections' for both the Waterline/Station intersection points, picked up from the Body Plan, and the Waterline/Buttock intersection points, picked up from the Profile View. All that remains is to re-fair the Waterlines using these corrected points.

As you can see from the drawing above, apart from the correction points, we're still using the Waterlines that were plotted earlier. (For clarity, the corrected lines are shown as dashed lines.)

We now have all three drawings relating to one another and can move on to plotting and drawing in the Diagonals which we'll use to check, and correct if necessary, the 'fairness' of all the lines we've drawn so far.

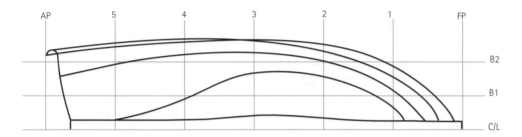

The drawing above shows the Half-breadth View with the corrected Waterlines drawn as a solid line (rather than the dashed line)

Fairing the Buttock Lines in the Profile View and then correcting any discrepancies that we find in the Body Plan and Half-breadth View may seem like a lot of work, but ultimately it's worth the effort. When we come to pick up and plot our Diagonals we can be confident that the information we're using is as accurate as possible, with all of the views relating to one another.

The next section of the book shows the range of techniques used to plot and fair the Diagonals and then carry out any final corrections to the Body Plan, Half-breadth View and Profile View.

PLOTTING AND FAIRING THE DIAGONALS

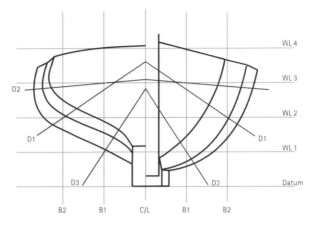

Once plotted and faired, Diagonals are used to correct any final discrepancies in the Body Plan. They're generally considered to be the most accurate lines because ideally they are drawn square to the Body Plan curve, almost as if they're following the line of the planking. In practice this is not possible, as all of the Stations have different curves, so a 'best-fit' line is drawn.

Diagonals are at their most effective in the area of the turn of the bilge (D1), and less so when they're almost horizontal (being similar to a Waterline, as shown in D2), or when they're almost vertical (being similar to a Buttock Line, as shown in D3).

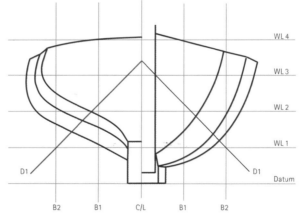

Diagonals can be drawn at any point, but to work correctly the Diagonal needs to start at a common point on the Body Plan C/L and move out at the same angle both sides of the C/L. In practice, this 'angle' is easy to achieve by drawing the Diagonal to pass through a common Waterline/Buttock Line intersection point, as shown in the above drawing.

Note: D1 (on both sides) starts at the C/L and passes through the same intersection point, in this case, WL 1 and B2.

The following pages will show the range of techniques used to pick up, plot and fair the Diagonals.

Step 1 (of 21)

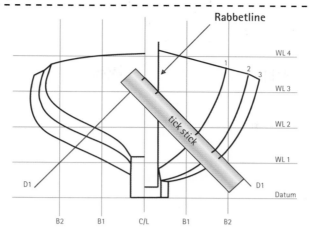

1 Using the same tick stick, we'll pick up the Diagonal intersection points on both the forward and aft Stations in the Body Plan.

2 Lay the tick stick along the Diagonal as shown in the drawing, using the C/L as a reference.

3 Pick up the Diagonal intersection points, in this case the Rabbetline and Stns 1, 2 and 3.

4 Move the tick stick to pick up the Diagonal intersection points in the aft section of the Body Plan, still using the same C/L reference mark.

Step 2

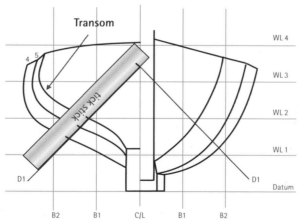

1 Lay the tick stick along the Diagonal as shown in the drawing, still using the C/L as a reference.

2 Pick up the remaining Diagonal intersection points, in this case Stns 4 and 5 and the Transom.

3 These intersection points will now be transferred to and plotted in the area beneath the Half-breadth View.

Step 3

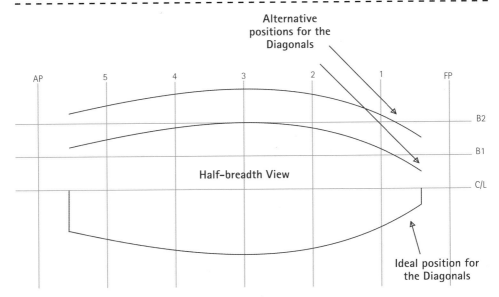

Alternative positions for the Diagonals

Half-breadth View

Ideal position for the Diagonals

In an ideal world, the Diagonals will be positioned below the Waterlines in the Half-breadth View, but if this isn't possible because of a lack of space, then they can be drawn in any of the positions shown above. However, this could make the final lofting drawing confusing, as they would be overlaying the existing Waterlines. As you can see above, the Diagonal can be drawn simply as a curved line, or the end points can be projected back to the C/L or a reference line; either way, it doesn't really affect the finished curve.

Step 4

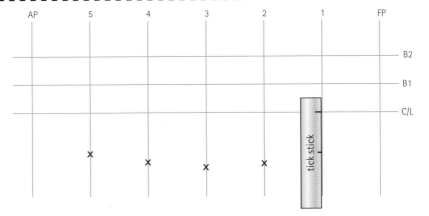

tick stick

1   Using the C/L as a reference, lay the tick stick on any Station, in this case Stn 1, and plot the Diagonal/Station intersection point, picked up in Steps 1 and 2, along the line as shown in the drawing above.

2   Repeat this process for all of the other Diagonal/Station intersection points picked up from the Body Plan. However, we can't plot the Rabbetline or the Transom points yet, as they need a little more information to be plotted correctly (see Step 5).

Step 5

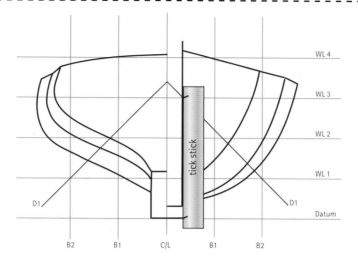

1   Use a tick stick – to avoid confusion, preferably a different one to the one used to collect the Diagonal/Station intersection points in Steps 1 and 2 – to find the 'height' of the Rabbetline/Diagonal intersection point in the Body Plan.

2   Lay the tick stick vertically along the Rabbetline, using either the Datum or any of the Waterlines as a reference, and pick up the intersection point as shown in the drawing.

3   Transfer this information to the Profile View.

Step 6

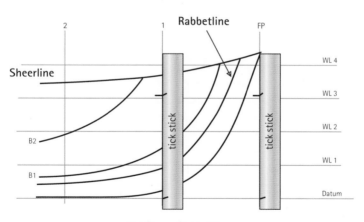

Profile or Sheer View

We now have two points which, when joined together, will show where in the Profile View, and then in the Half–breadth View, the Diagonal/Rabbetline intersection point is located

1   Lay the tick stick vertically along the FP, referencing off either the Datum or the Waterline that we used in Step 5.

2   Repeat this process at Stn 1.

Step 7

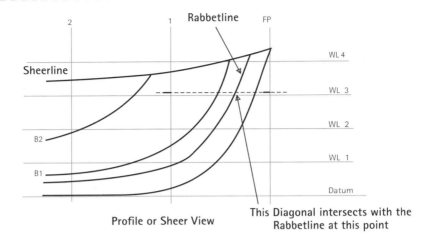

Rabbetline

FP

WL 4

Sheerline

WL 3

WL 2

B2

WL 1

B1

Datum

Profile or Sheer View

This Diagonal intersects with the Rabbetline at this point

1   Using a straight edge, join these two points together with a feint line.

2   Mark where this line intersects the Rabbetline.

3   This point is where this particular Diagonal intersects the Rabbetline in the Profile View.

In Step 8, we'll pick up this point and then transfer it to the Half-breadth View.

Step 8

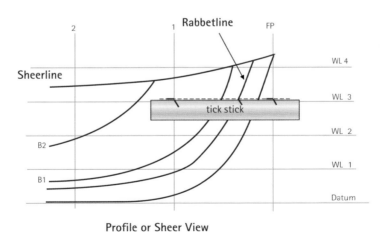

Rabbetline

FP

WL 4

Sheerline

WL 3

tick stick

WL 2

B2

WL 1

B1

Datum

Profile or Sheer View

1   Lay a tick stick along this line, using either the FP or Stn 1 as a reference.

2   Pick up the Rabbetline/Diagonal intersection point that we 'found' in Step 7.

3   Transfer this point to the Half-breadth View.

Step 9

1 Lay the tick stick on the C/L, using either the FP or Stn 1 as a reference, and transfer the intersection point picked up in Step 8 onto the C/L.

2 Repeat this process using either B1 or B2. In Step 10, we'll use these points to project a line, where the Rabbetline/Diagonal end point will be plotted.

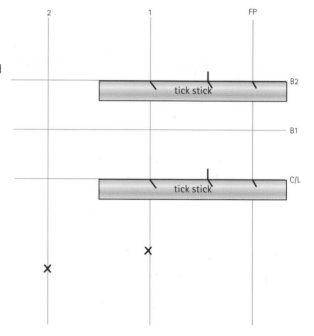

Step 10

1 Using a straight edge, join these two points together with a feint line, extending into the area where the Diagonal is being plotted.

2 The correct end point of the Diagonal/Rabbetline lies somewhere along this line.

The end point of the Diagonal with the Rabbetline lies somewhere along this line

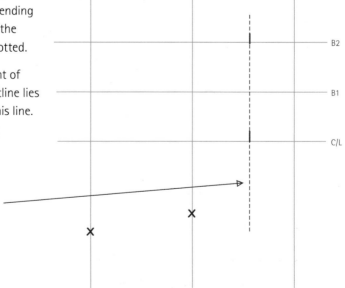

Step 11

1   Using the measurement for the Diagonal/Rabbetline intersection point, picked up in Step 1, lay the tick stick along the line, using the C/L as a reference, and transfer this point onto the line, as shown in the drawing on the right. This is the point where the forward part of the Diagonal ends.

2   We'll now use a similar set of techniques to find and plot the Diagonal end point with the Transom.

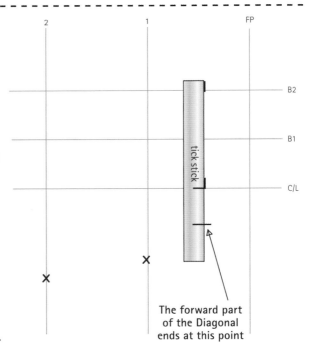

The forward part of the Diagonal ends at this point

Step 12

Next we need to find:

a)   The height above/below a reference line where the Diagonal intersects the Transom

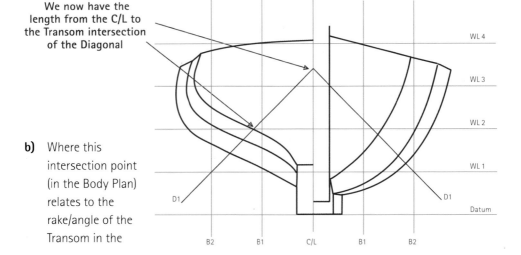

We now have the length from the C/L to the Transom intersection of the Diagonal

b)   Where this intersection point (in the Body Plan) relates to the rake/angle of the Transom in the

Profile View, and therefore where the Diagonal will end when plotted in the Half-breadth View

The following pages show the techniques used to find and plot this information.

Step 13

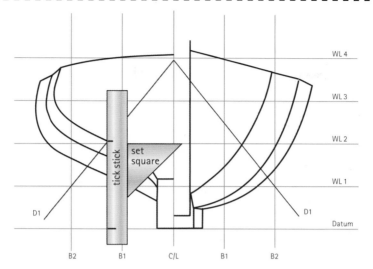

1   Use a set square or builder's square to make sure that the tick stick is aligned truly vertically.

2   Pick up the intersection 'height' of the Transom/Diagonal relative to any of the Waterlines or the Datum (in this case, we have used the Datum).

3   Transfer this 'height' to the Profile View to find out where the Diagonal will end.

Step 14

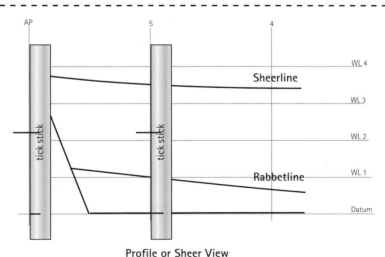

Profile or Sheer View

1   Lay the tick stick onto the AP, using the same reference as in Step 13, and transfer the Diagonal/Transom intersection 'height' onto the AP as shown in the drawing above.

2   Repeat this process at the next Station Line, in this case, Stn 5.

Step 15

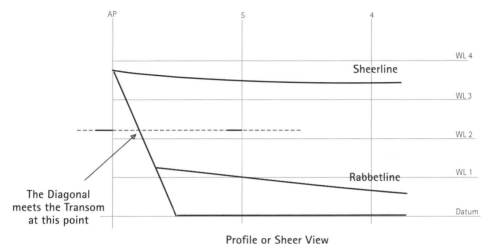

The Diagonal meets the Transom at this point

Profile or Sheer View

1   Join these two points together with a straight edge, and draw on a feint line.

2   This gives us the correct intersection point, in the Profile View, for where the Diagonal meets the Transom. We can then pick up and transfer this intersection point to the Half-breadth View.

Step 16

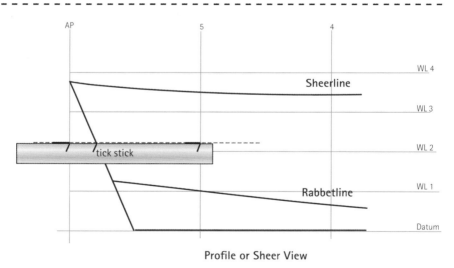

Profile or Sheer View

1   Lay a tick stick along the line, using either the AP or Stn 5 as a reference.

2   Pick up this Diagonal/Transom intersection point and then transfer it to the Half-breadth/Diagonal View.

Step 17

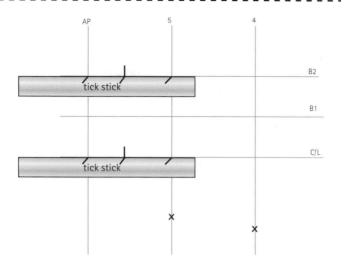

1   Lay the tick stick on the C/L, using either the AP or Stn 5 as a reference, and plot the Diagonal/Transom intersection point, picked up in Step 16, along the line as shown above.

2   Repeat this process using either B1 or B2.

In Step 18, we'll use these points to project a line where the Diagonal/Transom end point will be plotted.

Step 18

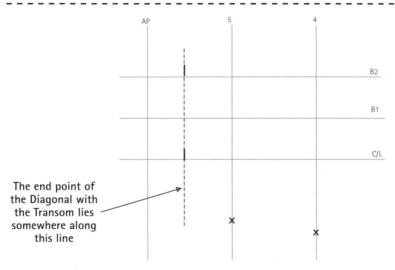

The end point of the Diagonal with the Transom lies somewhere along this line

1   Using a straight edge, join these points together with a feint line which projects out into the area where the Diagonal is being plotted.

2   The correct end point of the Diagonal/Transom lies somewhere along this line.

Step 19

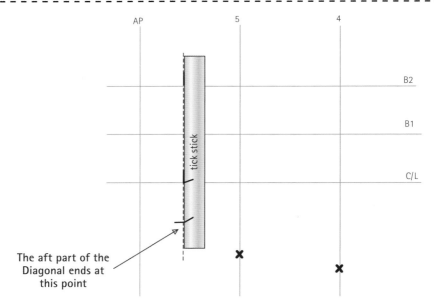

The aft part of the
Diagonal ends at
this point

1 Using the measurement for the Diagonal/Transom intersection point picked up in Step 2, lay the tick stick along the line drawn in Step 18, using the C/L as a reference, and transfer this point onto the line.

2 This gives us the final point needed to complete the first Diagonal.

Step 20

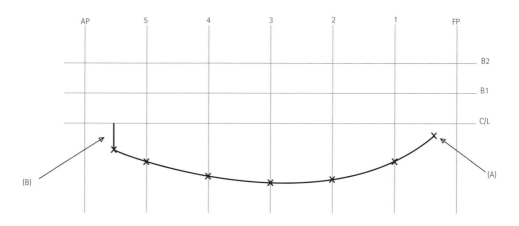

All that remains now is to join all of these points together with a batten to see how fair, or not, the Diagonal is. Then, as previously with the Buttock Lines, draw in all of the remaining Diagonals *before* making any corrections, to see if any 'error pattern' occurs. Note that at the ends we can either let the line finish on the end points or project a straight line back to the C/L; it doesn't really matter which we do, but personally I prefer to project the line back to the C/L.

Step 21

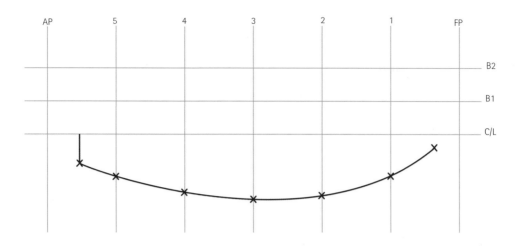

It's important to note that when drawing in the Diagonals, the line drawn needs to pass through all of the points we have plotted to check that what has been drawn in all of the other views is both fair and correct. If our line is fair and passes through all of the points, then we can assume that the rest of our lines are correct and we can confidently move on to the next stage in the lofting process, which is developing/expanding the Transom. However, if our Diagonal doesn't or can't pass through all of the points and still show as a fair line, then the final corrections will need to be carried out.

The next section deals with fairing the Diagonals and carrying out any final corrections to the other three views.

FAIRING THE DIAGONALS

Step 1 (of 14)

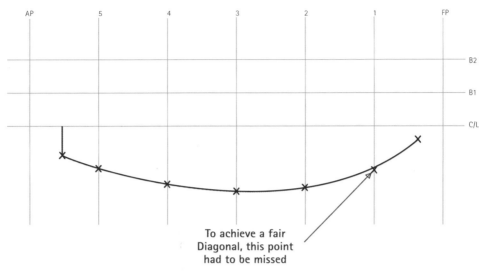

To achieve a fair
Diagonal, this point
had to be missed

If the Diagonal isn't fair, or to get a fair line, we need to miss one or more of the points (as shown in the example above), so we'll have to correct the Station Lines in the Body Plan (see Step 2). At this stage in the lofting process, any final corrections will usually be quite small because of the earlier corrections carried out after plotting and fairing the Buttock Lines.

Step 2

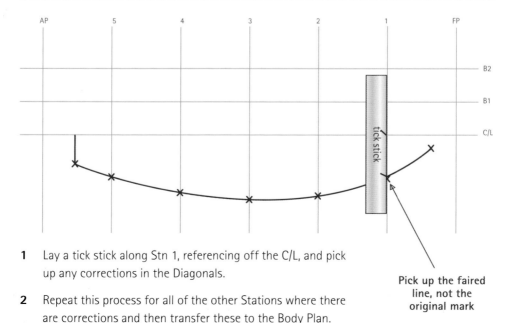

1   Lay a tick stick along Stn 1, referencing off the C/L, and pick
    up any corrections in the Diagonals.

Pick up the faired
line, not the
original mark

2   Repeat this process for all of the other Stations where there
    are corrections and then transfer these to the Body Plan.

Step 3

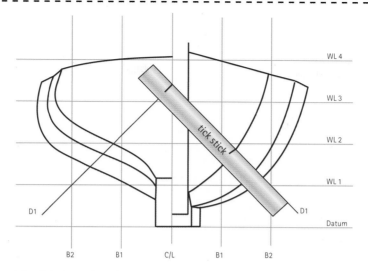

1. Lay the tick stick along D1, as shown in the drawing, and transfer any 'corrections' picked up from the Diagonal Half-breadths.

2. Repeat this process for all of the remaining Diagonals, both in the forward and aft sections of the Body Plan.

3. 'Re-fair' the Body Plan to the corrected Diagonals, which will then show up any final discrepancies in both the Waterline Half-breadths and the Buttock heights.

Step 4

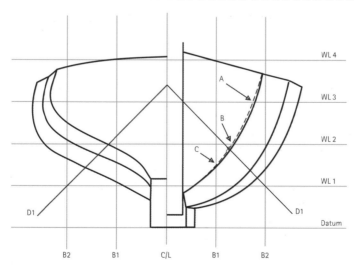

As you can see from the Body Plan, when we fair Stn 1 using the final correction to the Diagonal it has changed the following: the Half-breadth at WL 3; the Half-breadth at WL 2; the intersection height with B1. These discrepancies will now need to be transferred to, and corrected in, both the Half-breadth and the Profile Views.

Step 5

With the Body Plan completed, we can now carry out the final corrections to both the Half-breadth and the Profile Views, using similar techniques to those used earlier when plotting and fairing the Buttock Lines. The process to carry out the final corrections is outlined below:

1   Pick up the corrected Waterline Half-breadths from the Body Plan, transfer them to their corresponding Waterlines in the Half-breadth View and re-fair the Waterlines. This will show up any final discrepancies in the Half-breadth View Buttock/Waterline intersection points (see Steps 6 to 8).

2   Pick up these points and transfer them to the Waterline/Buttock intersections in the Profile View, but *don't* re-fair the Buttock Lines yet (see Steps 8 to 10).

3   Pick up the corrected Buttock heights from the Body Plan and transfer them to their corresponding Stations in the Profile View. We can now carry out the final fairing of the Buttock Lines in the Profile View (see Steps 11 to 13).

4   When all of these corrections have been completed, we should have four views (Profile, Half-breadth, Body Plan and Diagonal) where the measurements in one view relate to all the other views. We now have a fair hull.

5   With the hull faired, the next stage is to develop/expand the true shape of the Transom.

Step 6

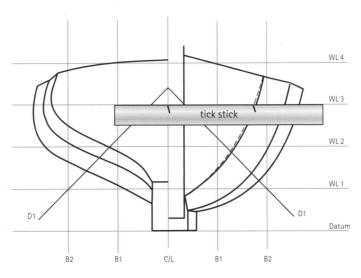

1   Lay the tick stick along WL 3, using the C/L as a reference, and pick up the 'corrected' Waterline Half-breadth.

2   Repeat this process on WL 2.

3   Transfer this information to the Half-breadth View.

Step 7

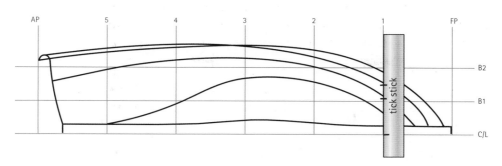

1 Lay the tick stick on Stn 1, using the C/L as a reference, and plot the final corrections to the Waterline Half-breadths, picked up in Step 6, onto the Station.

2 Repeat this process for any other Stations where final corrections to the Body Plan have been made and need to be transferred to the Half-breadth View.

3 Re-fair the Waterlines using these final corrections.

Step 8

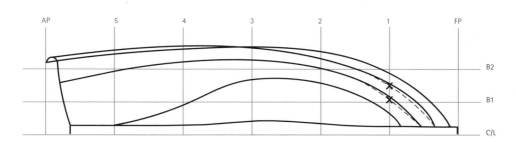

1 Using a batten, re-fair the Waterlines using these final corrections. (For clarity, the corrected lines are shown as dashed lines.) As you can see from the drawing above, apart from these corrections we're still using the Waterlines that were plotted earlier.

2 These corrected Waterlines will now show up any final discrepancies in the Waterline/ Buttock intersection points – in this case, where WL 2 and WL 3 intersect with B1.

3 Transfer these final corrections from the Half-breadth View to the Profile View.

Step 9

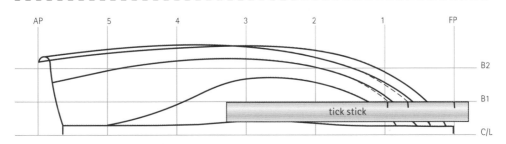

1   Lay the tick stick on B1, using the FP as a reference, and pick up the final corrections to the Waterline/Buttock intersection points plotted in Step 8.

2   Repeat this process for any of the other Buttocks where final corrections need to be made.

3   Transfer this information to the Profile View.

Step 10

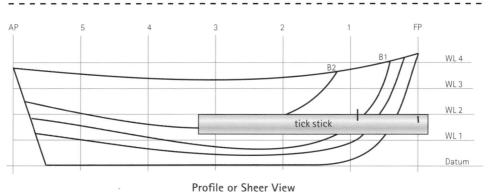

Profile or Sheer View

1   Lay a tick stick on WL 2, using the FP as a reference, and plot the final corrections to the Waterline/Buttock intersection point, picked up in Step 9, onto the Waterline.

2   Repeat this process for any of the other Waterlines where final corrections need to be made to the Buttock intersection point.

3   Do *not* re-fair the Buttock Lines in the Profile View yet (see Step 11).

Step 11

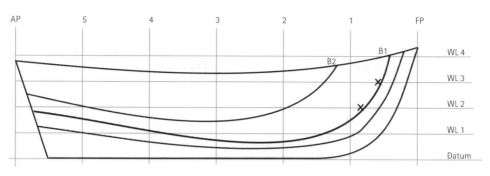

Profile or Sheer View

With the final corrections to the Waterline/Buttock intersection points plotted, all that remains is to pick up any final corrections to the Station/Buttock intersection points, plotted earlier in Step 4, and transfer them from the Body Plan to the Profile View.

Step 12

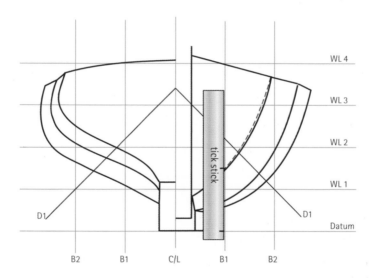

1. Lay the tick stick on B1, using the Datum as a reference, and pick up the final corrections to the Buttock/Station intersection points.

2. Repeat this process on any other Buttocks where final corrections to the Stations need to be made.

3. Transfer this information to the Profile View.

Step 13

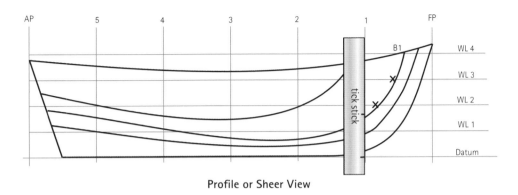

Profile or Sheer View

1   Lay the tick stick on Stn 1, using the Datum as a reference, and transfer the final correction to the Buttock/Station intersection point, picked up in Step 12, onto the Station.

2   Repeat this process for any other Stations where final Buttock corrections need to be made.

3   We now have all of the information needed to carry out the final fairing of the Buttock Lines in the Profile View.

Step 14

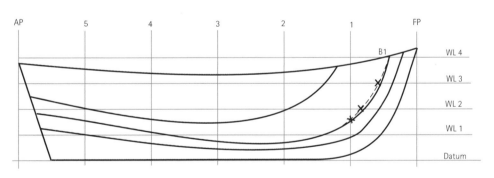

Profile or Sheer View

Using a fairing batten, join together all the final correction points plotted in the Profile View. As you can see from the drawing above, apart from the correction points we're still using the Buttock Lines plotted earlier. (For clarity, the corrected line is shown as a dashed line.) When all of these corrections have been completed, we should have four views (Profile, Half-breadth, Body Plan and Diagonals) where the measurements in one view relate to all the other views. We now have a fair hull.

EXPANDING/DEVELOPING THE TRANSOM

With all of the lines completed, we're now ready to develop the true shape and size of the Transom. If the boat has a plumb Transom, then its true shape is already drawn in the Body Plan.

Step 1 (of 7)

For a plumb Transom, this is the true shape and size of the aft face, not accounting for the thickness of the hull planking.

However, if we have a raked Transom, then we can't just use the Transom shape directly from the Body Plan. This is because although the Half-breadth measurements at the Sheer and Rabbetline and Waterlines are correct, the 'height' of a raked Transom is not 'true' in the Body Plan – the true height is found in the Profile View.

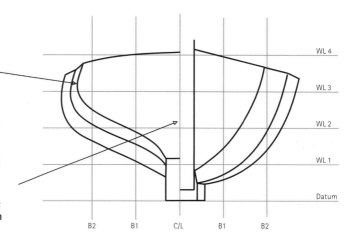

Step 2

This measurement is not the true 'height' of the raked Transom, as it does not take into account the angle at which the Transom is lying.

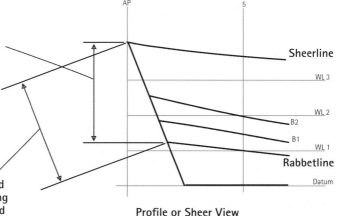

Profile or Sheer View

The true 'height' of the raked Transom is found by projecting two lines, from the Sheer and the Rabbetline, at 90 degrees to the Transom angle, as shown in the drawing. This then gives us the true Transom 'height'.

Step 3

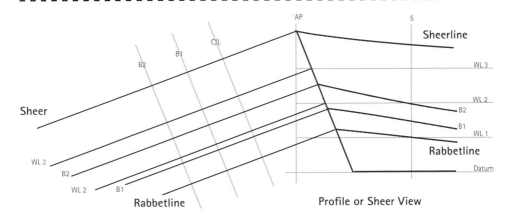

Sheer

WL 3

B2

WL 2 **B1**

Rabbetline

AP 5

Sheerline

WL 3

WL 2 **B2**

B1 WL 1

Rabbetline

Datum

Profile or Sheer View

1   To develop the true Transom shape, draw a line at 90 degrees to the Transom face for the Sheerline, Rabbetline and every Waterline or Buttock Line that ends on the Transom.

2   To make the final Transom expansion less confusing, draw a Transom 'expansion' C/L, parallel to the existing aft face of the Transom, as shown in the drawing above. Too many lines in this area close to the AP can lead to confusion.

3   Draw in the Transom 'expansion' Buttock Lines at their correct Half-breadth spacing, as shown in the drawing above.

4   Pick up the Transom Half-breadths, from the Body Plan, to plot them along the lines drawn above.

Step 4

1   Using the C/L as a reference, lay a tick stick along any one of the Waterlines, in this case WL 3, and pick up the Half-breadth of the Transom at that point. (For clarity, only the aft section of the Body Plan is shown here.)

2   Repeat this process for all of the other Waterlines, the Rabbetline and the Sheer.

3   Transfer these Transom lengths, or half-breadths, to the Transom development/ expansion.

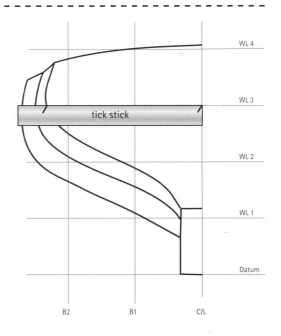

WL 4

WL 3

tick stick

WL 2

WL 1

Datum

B2 B1 C/L

Step 5

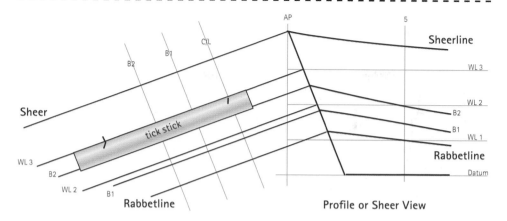

1   Using the C/L as a reference, lay the tick stick along any of the Waterlines, in this case WL 3, and plot the Waterline Half-breadth picked up in Step 4.

2   Repeat this process for all of the other Waterlines, the Rabbetline and the Sheer.

3   The technique for plotting the Buttock intersection points will be shown in Step 6.

Step 6

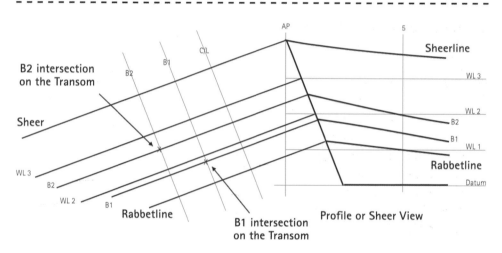

As the Buttock Half-breadths, measured out from the C/L, are known fixed lengths, all we need to do is find the co-ordinate points on the Transom development/expansion grid where B1 and B2 meet, as shown in the drawing above.

We now have all the information needed to develop the true 'expanded' shape of the Transom.

Step 7

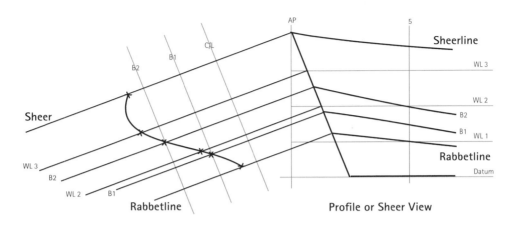

Sheerline

WL 3

WL 2

B2

B1 WL 1

Rabbetline

Datum

Sheer

WL 3

B2

WL 2 B1

Rabbetline

AP

5

CL

B1

B2

Profile or Sheer View

With all of the points plotted, use a flexible batten to develop the true 'expanded' shape of the Transom. However, this isn't the end of the Transom development. The Transom also has a Camber to its top surface; the general techniques used to develop this Camber, and how to transfer that information over to the Transom development/expansion, form the final part of this section of the book.

DEVELOPING A DECK CAMBER

Step 1 (of 5)

Details of the Deck Camber – also known as a 'beam crop' or a 'crown' – can usually be found in the Lines Plan or the construction drawing. The Camber in the drawing typically refers to the height of the deck above the Sheer at the maximum beam of the boat. The 'size' of the Camber is expressed as a 'height' above a Baseline, usually in inches or millimetres, in relation to a span, usually shown in feet or metres. For example, an imperial Camber may be shown as '4in in 8ft' while its metric equivalent may be shown as '100mm in 2.5m'. An example of a typical Deck Camber is shown below, with all of its main points identified.

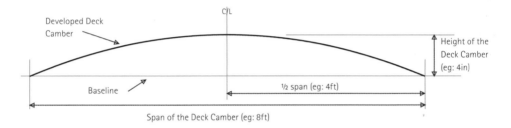

A Deck Camber can be developed using a form of trammel, or we can use a draughtsman's method. In practice, I've found that in the time it takes to source timber and construct the trammel we can have developed our Camber, using the draughtsman's method, directly onto the loft floor, and use that information to draw in the Camber of the Transom. The following page will show the method used to develop a Camber on the loft floor.

Step 2

The Deck Camber is usually developed using the half span, and then the resulting reference points are plotted on both sides, ie the full span. For this worked example, we're going to develop an imperial Deck Camber of 4in in 8ft. There are two reasons for this: firstly, it's quite a commonly used Camber; and secondly, as you'll see, these measurements are very easy to divide up – it makes it much better as a learning/teaching aid.

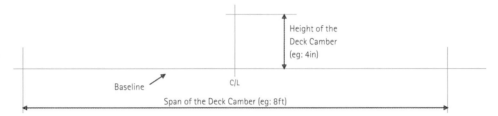

1   Set out the Baseline and put on two marks, 8ft apart.

2   Mark on the C/L position, and using either a set square or a pair of compasses, construct a vertical line at least 4in long.

3   Mark on the Deck Camber 'height', in this case 4in. Obviously this drawing isn't to scale.

4   With our reference lines set out, we're now ready to develop the actual Camber.

Step 3

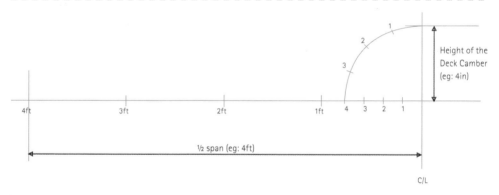

As mentioned earlier, the actual development uses the full height and the half span.

1   Divide the half-span Baseline into four equal parts, ie 1ft spacings.

2   With a pair of compasses, draw a quadrant with a Radius of 4in, using the C/L as a reference.

3   Divide the base of the quadrant into four equal parts, ie 1in spacings.

4   Divide the 'arc' into four equal parts, either with a protractor or by bisecting the angle.

5   We've created a proportional scale between the half span of the Baseline and the quadrant/Deck Camber height. In Step 4 we'll use the proportional scale of the quadrant to determine the intermediate Camber heights in the half span.

Step 4

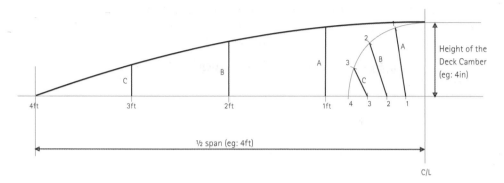

1   In the quadrant, join together the points along the Baseline with the points around the arc, ie 1 to 1, 2 to 2 etc. As you can see from the drawing, we now have three lines slanted at varying angles.

2   Using a tick stick, pick up these slope lengths A, B and C and transfer them to the half-span Baseline.

3   Project these lengths vertically upwards at the 1ft, 2ft and 3ft positions, both on the left-hand side (shown below) and on the right-hand side (not shown in this drawing).

4   Using a batten, plot a line going through all of the points to give us a fair Deck Camber.

Note: It might seem as if the process of creating a Deck Camber this way is very time-consuming. It isn't: in practice, the whole thing can be done in 5–10 minutes.

Step 5

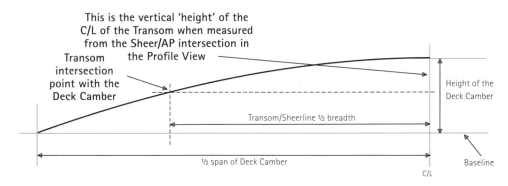

This is the vertical 'height' of the
C/L of the Transom when measured
from the Sheer/AP intersection in
the Profile View

Transom
intersection
point with the
Deck Camber

Height of the
Deck Camber

Transom/Sheerline ½ breadth

½ span of Deck Camber

Baseline

C/L

In an ideal world, the vertical height of the Transom at the C/L will be shown on either the Offset Table or the Lines Plan. If this information is not shown we can use the Deck Camber we've just drawn to find this height. For clarity, this technique will be shown using the half-span Deck Camber (see the drawing below).

1   Using the C/L as a reference, mark the Transom Sheerline Half-breadth onto the Baseline.

2   Then, using a set square or builder's square, project this point up until it intersects the Deck Camber.

3   Draw a horizontal line from this point back to intersect the C/L.

4   The distance between this intersection point and the top of the Deck Camber is the vertical 'height' – above the Sheer/AP intersection point – of the Transom at the C/L of the boat. This point can now be transferred to the AP in the Profile View and used to draw in the true Transom Deck Camber. The techniques to do this are shown in the following pages.

DEVELOPING THE TRANSOM DECK CAMBER

Step 1 (of 10)

As mentioned earlier, in an ideal world the vertical height of the Transom C/L will be found either in the Offset Table or on the Lines Plan. If this is the case, then all we need to do is to plot this vertical height onto the AP, above the Transom/Sheerline intersection point, and then carry on with developing the Transom Deck Camber (see Step 3). However, if we haven't got this information, it means we'll need to construct a Deck Camber twice: once to find the height of the Transom C/L and plot it onto the AP, and then a second time to develop the correct Transom Deck Camber, with the Camber C/L based in the correct position (see Step 3).

The reason for this is that any Half-breadth measurements always need to be taken from the C/L of the Deck Camber. The further out from the C/L the Camber moves, the steeper the curved line becomes. The three drawings below clearly show why we would need to do this. In each of the drawings the Transom/Sheerline Half-breadth is the same 'length', but where it has been referenced from along the Baseline is different in order to show how the 'height' could vary. These drawings clearly show that in order to achieve consistency in our boat's Camber any development must use the Camber C/L as a reference. Hopefully, any boat we come to loft will have the Transom C/L height, but if it doesn't and we have to develop the Deck Camber twice, it'll only take us an extra 5–10 minutes for the second Camber development.

Step 2

1   Using the C/L as a reference gives us the 'height' shown in this drawing – this is the correct vertical height that we'll use to develop the true Transom Deck Camber.

2   Keeping the Half-breadth measurement (X) the same, but moving it further out from the C/L, gives us a greater vertical height.

3   In this example, the Half-breadth (X) has started at the far end of the Deck Camber and we've measured back in towards the C/L. As you can see, this gives us an even greater height and shows why, for consistency, the Camber needs to reference from the C/L.

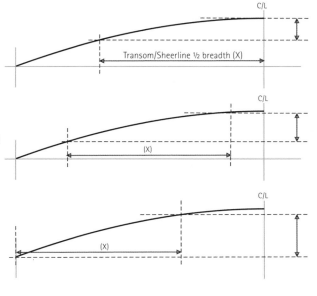

Step 3

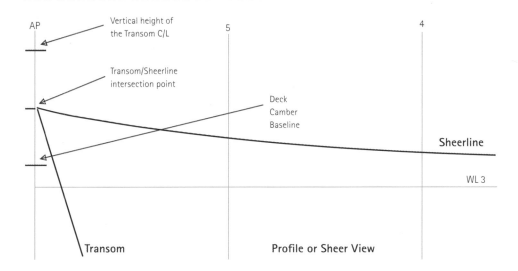

1 Using the Transom/Sheerline intersection point as an initial reference, plot the vertical height of the Transom C/L onto the AP.

2 Measuring *down* from this point, plot the designated 'height' of the full Deck Camber to give us our Baseline.

We'll use these three points to develop both our full Deck Camber and the Transom Deck Camber.

Step 4

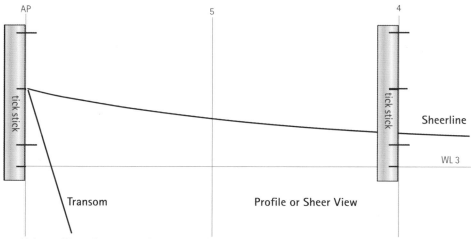

1 Using a Waterline as a reference, in this case WL 3, lay a tick stick along the AP and pick up the height of the Transom C/L, the Transom/Sheerline intersection point and the Baseline position of the Deck Camber.

2 Transfer this information over to a Station Line, in this case Stn 4, and, using WL 3 as a reference, plot these points onto the Station.

Step 5

1   Using a straight edge, join together these three sets of points with a feint line – shown as a dashed line for clarity – to give us the framework for our Deck Camber development.

2   Using the techniques described earlier, develop a Deck Camber, using Stn 4 as the C/L. (For clarity, only half of the Deck Camber has been shown.)

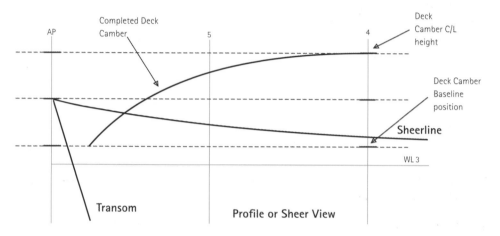

Step 6

1   Using Stn 4 (C/L) as a reference, plot the Half-breadths of B1 and B2 etc along the Sheer intersection line.

2   Project these points up vertically until they intersect with the Deck Camber.

We now have the information needed to develop the Transom Deck Camber accurately.

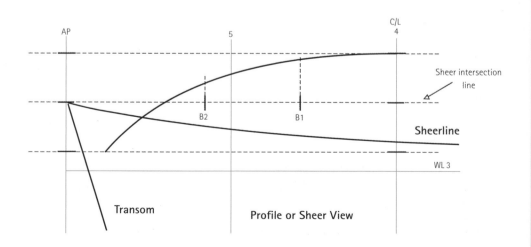

Step 7

1 Using a tick stick, pick up the Camber intersection points B1 and B2, using the Sheer intersection line as a reference.

2 Using the same reference line, plot these points onto the AP.

3 Join these points together using a feint line and extend the lines past the AP as shown in the drawing below.

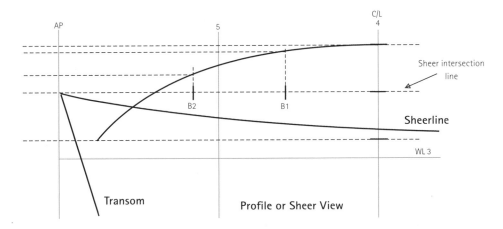

Step 8

1 As this boat has a raked Transom, the lines we have drawn at B1, B2 and the Transom C/L height need to be projected out at 90 degrees, in the same way that all of the other Transom Half-breadths have been. But where exactly do we do this?

2 Extend the raked Transom angle upwards, using a feint line. Where it intersects with B1, B2 and the Transom C/L height is where the lines will project out at 90 degrees.

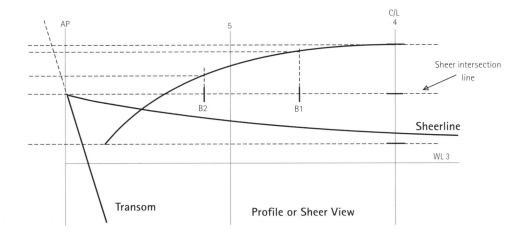

Step 9

Where the C/L 'height', B1 and B2 intersect the extended angle of the Transom, a line is projected out at 90 degrees.

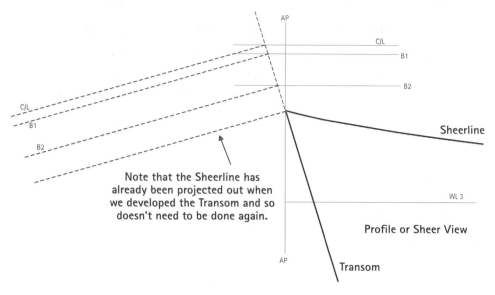

Note that the Sheerline has already been projected out when we developed the Transom and so doesn't need to be done again.

All that remains now is to connect these points in the Transom expansion/development to create the true shape of the Transom Deck Camber.

Step 10

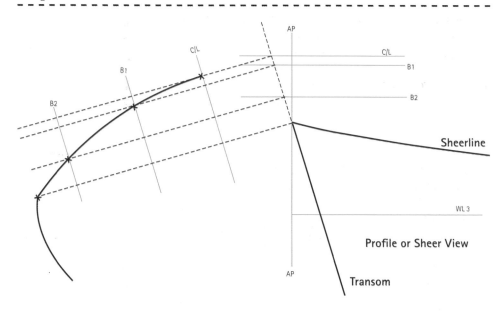

Where our projected lines C/L, B1 and B2 intersect their respective lines in the Transom expansion we put down a mark (X), and then, using a batten, join the points together, giving us the true development of the Transom Deck Camber. Obviously this drawing is not to scale.

CONGRATULATIONS!
THE BASIC LOFTING OF
THE BOAT IS COMPLETE

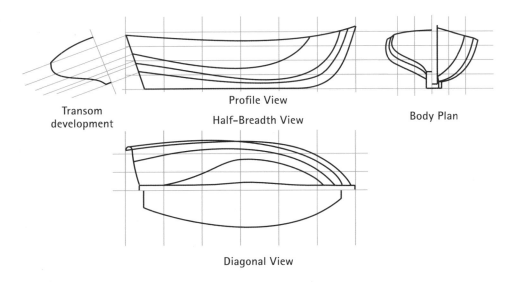

Transom
development

Profile View

Half–Breadth View

Body Plan

Diagonal View

With everything completed, the finished lofting should look similar to this, depending on the design of boat that you've chosen. If all you wanted to do was create a full-size Lines Drawing, I'm pleased to say that you've finished – time to have a drink! However, if you want to take this to the next stage in order to actually build the boat, then some additional work needs to be done. An outline of Part 2, which deals with this, is shown on the opposite page.

WHAT NEXT?

With the basic lofting completed, we're now ready to work on Part 2 of this process, which covers the stages outlined below using the same step-by-step methods employed previously:

- Developing the forward face of a raked/angled Transom (to accommodate for the thickness of the Transom)

- Lofting a boat with a Radiused Transom. This covers developing both the forward and the aft face of a Radiused Transom using two of the most common ways of designing this style of Transom

- Developing the Keel cross-sections

- Stem Bevel/cross-section development

- Scantlings (Moulding and Siding – how do we use this information?)

- Accounting for planking thickness (two methods)

- Taking frame/Station bevels and creating a Bevel Board

- Picking up templates and patterns from the loft floor

There is also a very detailed project costing sheet (available as a free download from my website www.streamandshore.com). This covers all of the stages involved in planning, building and fitting out a wooden boat, helping you to get a clear idea of the costs involved before starting your build. This allows accurate budgeting for each stage of the build. Remember, most boatbuilding projects fail because of a lack of money, *not* enthusiasm or skill!

PART TWO

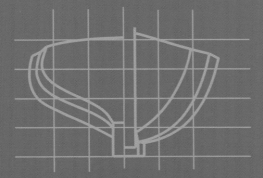

DEVELOPING THE FORWARD FACE OF A RAKED/ANGLED TRANSOM

Step 1 (of 7)

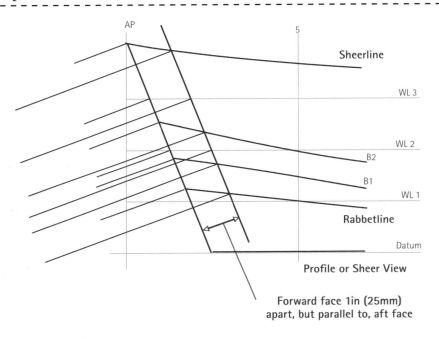

Profile or Sheer View

Forward face 1in (25mm)
apart, but parallel to, aft face

Using information either from the drawings, Scantlings (see page 126) or from a similar boat, draw the forward face of the Transom, ie its thickness, onto the Profile View. In this example we'll assume that the Transom has a thickness of 1in (25mm).

1 Draw a line parallel to the aft face but 1in (25mm) forward of it – as you can see from the drawing, this is measured 'square' to the angled face and not along the Waterline.

2 As with the aft face, project lines out at 90° to the Transom's forward face where the Sheer, Rabbetline and Waterlines intersect the Transom.

Note that with a typical 'aft-raked' Transom the projected lines from the forward face will be parallel to, but below, the lines projected from the aft face (see the drawing above).

Step 2

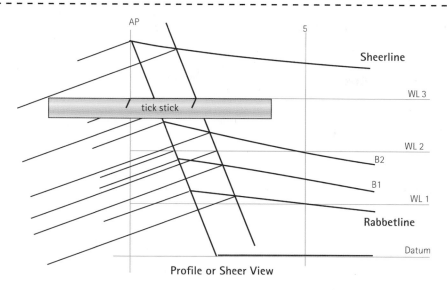

Profile or Sheer View

We now need to find the Half-breadth, or width, of the forward face of the Transom where it intersects both the Waterlines and the Sheerline. Remember that as with the aft face, the Buttock Half-breadths are already known.

1. Lay the tick stick along WL 3 as shown in the drawing and pick up the positions of the AP and the forward face of the Transom.

2. Transfer this information to the Half-breadth View to determine the actual Half-breadth of WL 3 at the forward face of the Transom.

Step 3

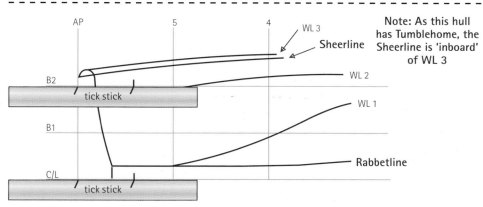

Using the AP as a reference, lay the tick stick along the C/L and transfer the intersection point picked up in Step 2 onto the C/L.

Repeat this process using one of the Buttock Lines, in this case B2. In Step 4 we'll use these points to project a line to determine the actual Half-breadth (width) of the Transom's forward face at WL 3.

Step 4

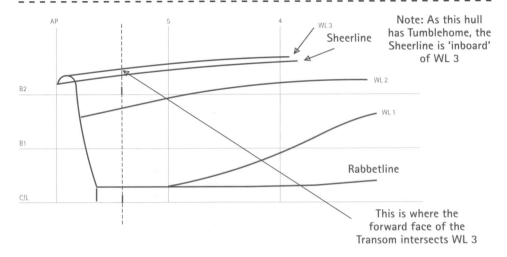

Note: As this hull has Tumblehome, the Sheerline is 'inboard' of WL 3

This is where the forward face of the Transom intersects WL 3

1 Using a straight edge, join these two points together with a feint line.

2 Where this line intersects WL 3 is the actual Half-breadth of WL 3 at the forward face of the Transom. In Step 5, we'll see how to pick up and transfer this information.

Step 5

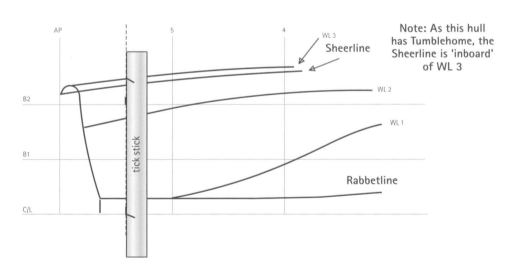

Note: As this hull has Tumblehome, the Sheerline is 'inboard' of WL 3

1 Lay a tick stick along the line and pick up the C/L and the point where the line intersects WL 3.

2 Transfer this information to the Transom development area of the Profile View.

Step 6

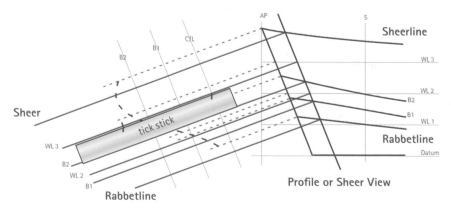

Sheer

tick stick

Rabbetline

AP   5

Sheerline

WL 3

WL 2

B2

B1   WL 1

Rabbetline

Datum

Profile or Sheer View

1   Using the C/L as a reference, lay the tick stick along WL 3 and plot the Waterline Half-breadth picked up in Step 5.

2   Repeat this process for all of the other Waterlines, the Rabbetline and the Sheer.

Please note, as with the aft face of the Transom, the Buttock positions are plotted using the intersection points. For clarity, the existing lines/development of the aft face are shown as dotted lines.

Step 7

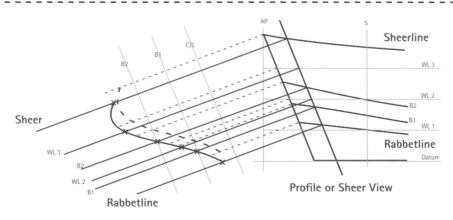

Sheer

Rabbetline

AP   5

Sheerline

WL 3

WL 2

B2

B1   WL 1

Rabbetline

Datum

Profile or Sheer View

With all of the points plotted, use a flexible batten to develop the true shape of the forward face of the Transom. As we can see from the drawing, the forward face of a raked/angled Transom is 'larger' than the aft face, and its development is 'below' that of the aft face – don't worry, this is normal. Note that if the boat is lofted to the outside of the hull, we'll still need to make an allowance for plank thickness; this will be dealt with later when we look at making Mould Stations.

Some of the most beautiful boats ever built have a Radiused Transom, and the range of techniques used to develop a Radiused Transom form the next section of the book.

LOFTING A RADIUSED TRANSOM

Up to now we've looked at lofting a boat with a flat/raked Transom. When we loft a boat with a Radiused Transom we need to modify the order in which we do things and then add in a range of specialised techniques. Many people are afraid to loft a boat with a Radiused Transom but, as with all of the techniques used so far, it's simply a question of working in a methodical manner.

There are two main methods for lofting a Radiused Transom:

1   Where the Transom is drawn perpendicular to the angle of the Transom

2   Where the Transom is drawn along the Waterlines

For both of these methods, we can't draw in the Sheerline in the Profile View until we have determined exactly where the Sheerline will end. By first of all drawing in the Transom in the Body Plan – but none of the other Stations – we can find the 'height' of the Sheerline; if we transfer this 'height' to the Profile View we can create a horizontal line along which we know the Sheerline will end. This is a common technique that's used for both methods of lofting a Radiused Transom. When this line has been drawn in, we can then use whichever method is needed, depending on the original designer, to draw the Radiused Transom in both the Profile View and the Half-breadth View. When these lines have been completed, we can then carry on lofting the boat using exactly the same basic techniques already used to loft a boat with a flat/raked Transom.

Next we'll need to expand/develop the Radiused Transom. Unlike a flat/raked Transom, when we expand/develop the Radiused Transom we need to take into account the curvature of the Transom and, in effect, 'unwrap' the Transom as we develop it. This will enable us to create templates later on to actually make the Transom. The techniques used differ slightly depending on which method the designer chose to create the Radiused Transom, but the following pages show both methods, using the same step-by-step techniques seen previously.

As I promised at the beginning of the book, I'll try to keep the words to a minimum and the drawings to a maximum, so let's get on and start lofting a Radiused Transom!

LOFTING A BOAT WITH A RADIUSED TRANSOM – A COMMON FIRST STAGE

Step 1 (of 4)

1   Following the same techniques employed earlier, plot the Transom in the Body Plan using information obtained from the Offset Table.

2   Using a set square to ensure that the tick stick is aligned in a truly vertical manner, pick up the height of the Transom and any Waterline, in this case WL 3, to use as a reference.

3   Transfer this information to the Profile View.

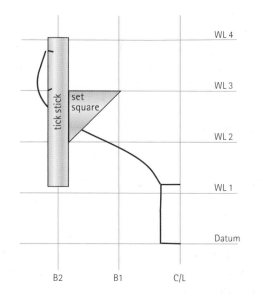

Step 2

1   Lay the tick stick vertically on the AP, using WL 3 as a reference, and plot the Transom Sheer height, picked up in Step 1, onto the AP.

2   Repeat this process using the next available Station Line, in this case Stn 5.

In Step 3 we'll use these points to project a line along which the Sheerline will end.

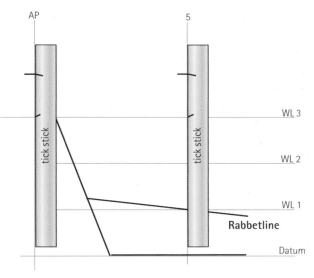

Profile or Sheer View

Step 3

1   Using a straight edge, join these points together with a feint line.

2   The correct end position of the Sheerline in the Profile View lies somewhere along this line.

As mentioned earlier, this technique is common to both methods of lofting and developing a Radiused Transom, and Step 4 involves the final common technique.

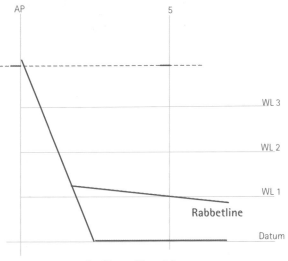

Profile or Sheer View

Step 4

1   Using the C/L as a reference, lay a tick stick along any one of the Waterlines, in this case WL 3, and pick up the Half-breadth of the Transom at that point.

2   Repeat this process for all of the other Waterlines, the Rabbetline, the Sheer and the Buttock Lines.

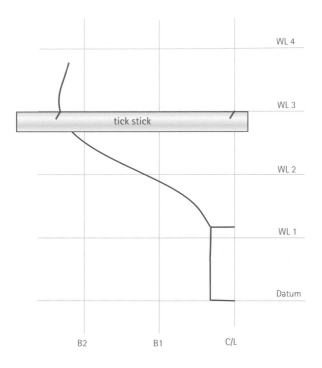

This 'common' set of information is now used in different ways, depending on the method required to loft the Radiused Transom. The following pages will deal firstly with a Transom radiused perpendicular to the angle of the Transom, and secondly with a Transom that is radiused along the Waterlines.

LOFTING THE AFT FACE OF A RADIUSED TRANSOM, WHERE THE TRANSOM IS DEVELOPED PERPENDICULAR TO THE TRANSOM ANGLE

Step 1 (of 8)

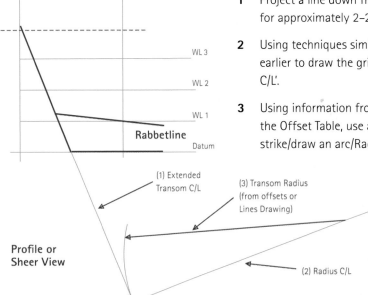

Profile or Sheer View

1 Project a line down from the Transom C/L for approximately 2–2.5m (6–8ft).

2 Using techniques similar to those used earlier to draw the grid, project a 'Radius C/L'.

3 Using information from the Lines Plan or the Offset Table, use a set of trammels to strike/draw an arc/Radius as shown below.

Using WL 3 as a worked example, we'll now determine how to draw the Radiused Transom in the Profile View.

Step 2

1 Using a tick stick, pick up the Half-breadth of WL 3 (see step 4 of the 'common first stage').

2 Lay the tick stick along the extended Transom C/L.

3 Transfer the Half-breadth of WL 3 onto the extended Transom C/L.

We'll now use this information to construct a line connecting the extended Transom C/L to the Transom Radius arc.

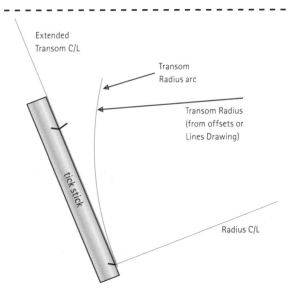

Step 3

1   Use a set square to ensure that the tick stick is aligned perpendicular to the extended Transom C/L.

2   Lay the tick stick so that it intersects both the extended Transom C/L and the Transom Radius arc.

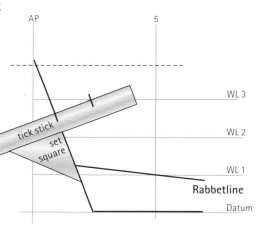

3   Pick up these two intersection points (as shown in the drawing).

4   Transfer this information to the Profile View to determine the intersection point of the Radiused Transom with WL 3.

Step 4

1   Use a set square to ensure that the tick stick lies perpendicular to the Transom C/L.

2   Position the tick stick, as shown in the drawing, so that the two marks transferred from Step 3 intersect with both the Transom C/L and WL 3.

3   Plot this point onto WL 3. This gives us the position of the aft face of the Radiused Transom at WL 3.

4   Repeat this process for the remaining Waterlines, the Rabbetline and the Sheerline.

Profile or Sheer View

Step 5

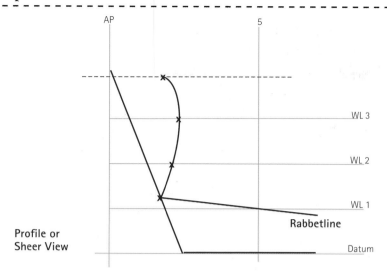

Profile or Sheer View

1   With all of the points plotted, we can then join them together with a flexible batten.

2   This gives us the shape of the aft face of the Radiused Transom.

3   We can now determine the Transom intersection points of the Buttock Lines. The technique used is practically identical to that used for a flat/raked Transom, except that the Buttock Line ends at the Transom itself and not at the Transom C/L.

Step 6

1   Using the same techniques employed earlier for a flat/raked Transom, lay a tick stick along B1, using either the Datum or any other Waterline as a reference.

2   Mark the Buttock/Transom intersection 'height' onto the tick stick.

3   Repeat this process for the remaining Buttock/Transom intersection 'heights', in this case B2.

4   Transfer this information to the Profile View.

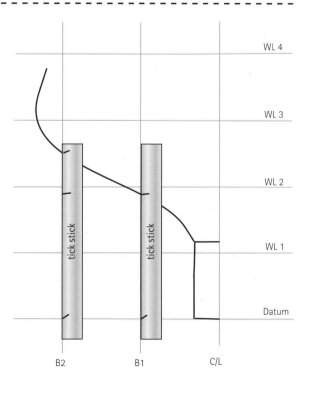

Step 7

1. Lay the tick stick along the AP, using the Datum, or your Waterline, as a reference, and transfer the 'heights' of B1 and B2 onto the AP.

2. Repeat this process at the next Station, in this case Stn 5.

3. We can now join these points together to show the intersection points of B1 and B2 with the Radiused Transom.

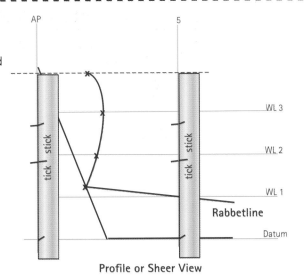

Profile or Sheer View

Step 8

1. Using a straight edge, join together these two sets of points with a feint line.

2. The points at which these feint lines intersect the Radiused Transom are the end positions of B1 and B2 in the Profile View.

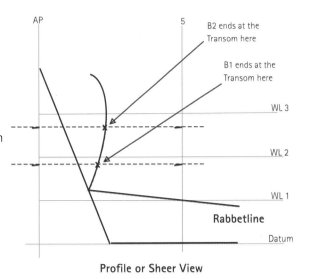

Profile or Sheer View

With the Transom/Buttock intersection points plotted, we can now carry on lofting the boat using exactly the same techniques employed earlier for lofting a boat with a flat/raked Transom.

We'll now move on to expanding/developing the Radiused Transom to show its true size and shape, taking into account the Transom curvature.

EXPANDING/DEVELOPING THE AFT FACE OF A RADIUSED TRANSOM, WHERE THE TRANSOM IS DEVELOPED PERPENDICULAR TO THE TRANSOM ANGLE

Step 1 (of 4)

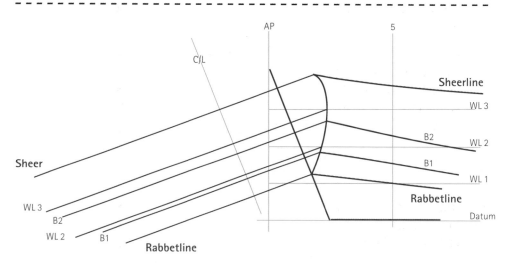

Profile or Sheer View

1   As with a flat/raked Transom, lines are drawn at 90 degrees to the angle of the Transom C/L but they start at the intersection of the Radiused Transom and various lines (eg WL 3, B2 etc).

2   As with a flat/raked Transom, we again draw in an expansion C/L, but *not* B1 and B2, as will be explained in Steps 2 and 3.

Step 2

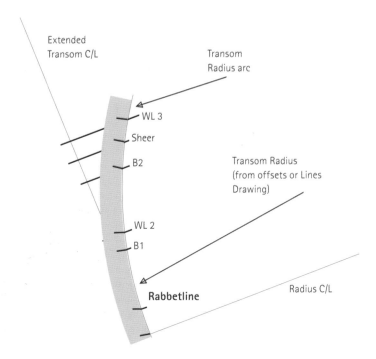

Extended
Transom C/L

Transom
Radius arc

WL 3

Sheer

B2

Transom Radius
(from offsets or Lines
Drawing)

WL 2

B1

Rabbetline

Radius C/L

1   Lay a 'flexible' batten or tick stick around the Transom Radius arc and pick up the 'squared over' Half-breadths – this batten/tick stick will probably need to be temporarily secured in place using either 'spline weights' or nails.

2   These points will then be transferred to and plotted on the expanded Transom grid created in Step 1.

3   As you can probably see, when we transfer these points we'll 'unwrap' the flexible batten/tick stick so that the spacings between the points will be wider than in the Body Plan, as the Body Plan doesn't take into account the curvature/Radius of the Transom and doesn't represent the true size or shape of the Radiused Transom.

Step 3

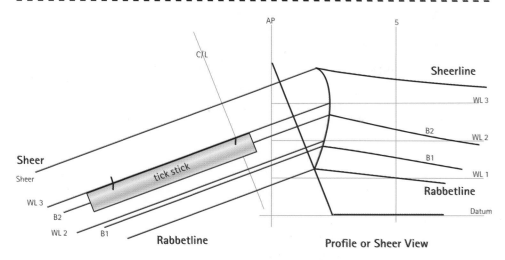

1   Taking WL 3 as a worked example, and using the C/L as a reference, unwrap the flexible batten/tick stick and transfer the curved Half-breadth, picked up in Step 2, onto the Transom expansion line as shown in the drawing.

2   Repeat this process for the remaining Waterlines, Buttock Lines, Sheerline and Rabbetline.

Step 4

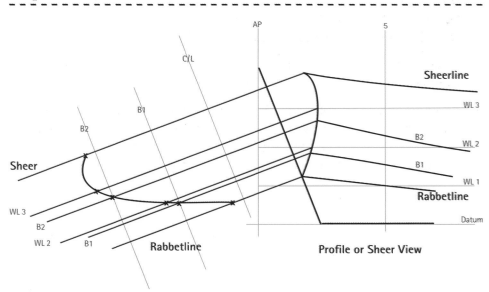

1   With all of the points plotted, use a flexible batten to develop the true 'expanded' aft face of the Radiused Transom.

2   Due to the 'unwrapping', the Buttocks appear wider apart in this view than in the Body Plan. This is normal for a Radiused Transom, the spacing depending upon the Radius of the Transom.

EXPANDING/DEVELOPING THE FORWARD FACE OF A RADIUSED TRANSOM, WHERE THE TRANSOM IS DEVELOPED PERPENDICULAR TO THE TRANSOM ANGLE

Using WL 3 as a worked example, we'll now look at the techniques used to develop/expand the forward face of a Radiused Transom. Please note that this can't be done until the whole boat has been lofted.

Step 1 (of 9)

As with a flat/raked Transom, draw a line parallel to the Transom C/L, but forward of it by the thickness of the Transom, and extend the line down to the Radius C/L.

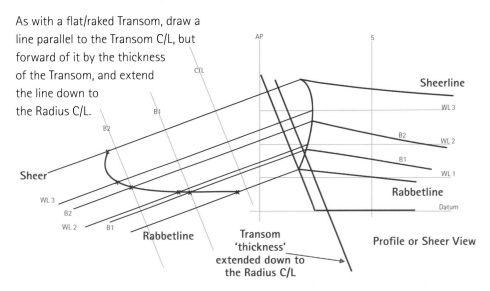

Profile or Sheer View

Step 2

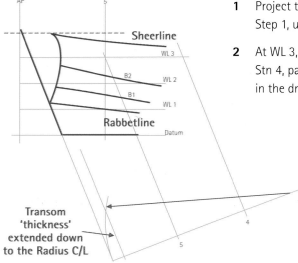

1   Project the 'Transom thickness' line, from Step 1, until it intersects the Radius C/L.

2   At WL 3, project down lines at Stn 5 and Stn 4, parallel to the Transom C/L, as shown in the drawing.

3   Along these two lines – Stns 5 and 4 – we'll then plot the Half-breadth of WL 3, taken from the completed Half-breadth View, and connect these points through to the Radius Half-breadth of WL 3 that we already have.

Step 3

1 Using the WL 3 Half-breadths for Stns 4 and 5 and WL 3 on the aft face of the Radiused Transom, join these points together as shown below to create a line showing the Half-breadth of WL 3.

2 Using the same 'Radius origin', draw an arc for the forward face of the Transom, as shown below, that intersects the line we have just drawn. This intersection point is where the forward face of the Transom meets WL 3, and we can use this information to determine both the forward face of WL 3 in the Profile View and the correct developed/expanded Half-breadth of WL 3 on the Transom's forward face.

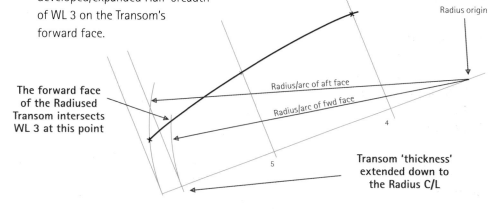

Radius origin

Radius/arc of aft face

Radius/arc of fwd face

The forward face of the Radiused Transom intersects WL 3 at this point

Transom 'thickness' extended down to the Radius C/L

Step 4

1 Use a set square to ensure that the tick stick is aligned perpendicular to the extended Transom C/L.

2 Lay the tick stick so that it intersects both the extended Transom C/L and the intersection of WL 3 and the Transom Radius arc (forward face).

Extended Transom C/L

WL 3

tick stick

set square

Transom Radius arc (fwd face)

Radius C/L

3 Pick up these intersection points as shown in the drawing.

4 Transfer this information to the Profile View to determine the intersection point of the forward face of the Radiused Transom with WL 3.

Step 5

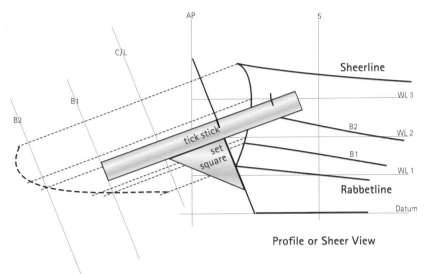

Profile or Sheer View

Note: For clarity, the existing lines/development of the aft face are shown here as dotted lines.

1. As previously with the aft face, lay the set square/tick stick so that it lies on the Radiused Transom C/L and intersects WL 3 as shown. This gives us the forward face of the Transom at WL 3.

2. Repeat this process for the remaining Waterlines, Sheerline and Rabbetline.

Step 6

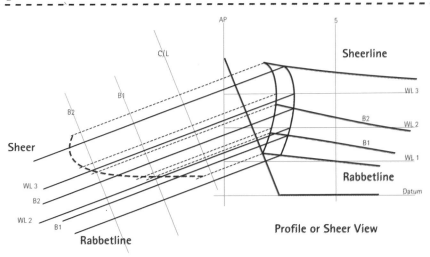

Profile or Sheer View

1. With the forward face of the Transom plotted in the Profile View, we can now project lines at 90 degrees to the Radiused Transom's C/L, where the forward face of the Transom intersects with the Sheerline, Rabbetline and Waterlines.

2 Note that, as with a flat/raked Transom, the lines of the forward face are parallel to, but below the lines of, the aft face.

3 As with the aft face, we can pick up the Radius intersection points and 'unwrap' them along their respective lines.

Step 7

1 Using WL 3 as a worked example, lay a 'flexible' batten or tick stick around the Transom Radius arc (forward face) and pick up the Radius C/L and the intersection point of WL 3 with the Transom Radius arc (forward face). As with the aft face, this batten/tick stick will probably need to be temporarily secured in place, using either spline weights or nails.

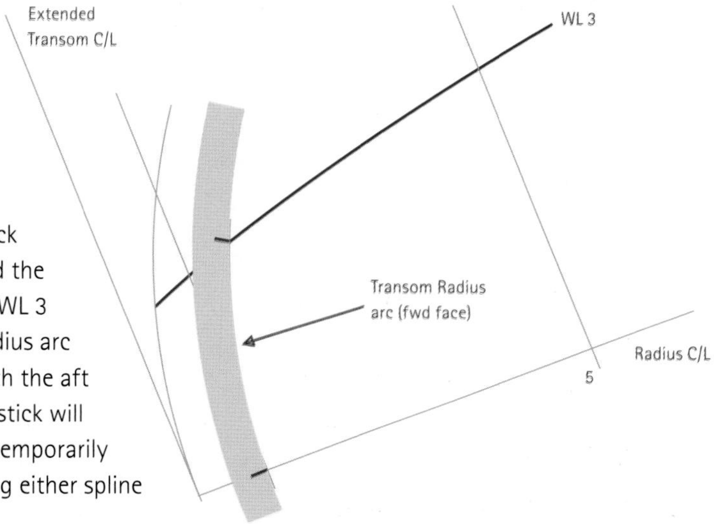

Extended Transom C/L

WL 3

Transom Radius arc (fwd face)

Radius C/L

5

2 These points will then be transferred to and plotted on the expanded Transom grid created earlier.

Step 8

1   Taking WL 3 as a worked example, and using the C/L as a reference (using the same technique as before), unwrap the flexible batten/tick stick and transfer the curved Half-breadth (picked up in Step 7) onto the Transom expansion line as shown in the drawing.

2   Repeat this process for the remaining Waterlines, Buttock Lines, Sheerline and Rabbetline.

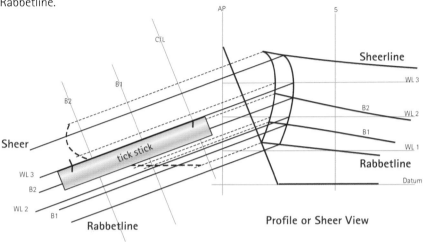

Step 9

With all of the points plotted, use a flexible batten to develop the true 'expanded' forward face of the Radiused Transom.

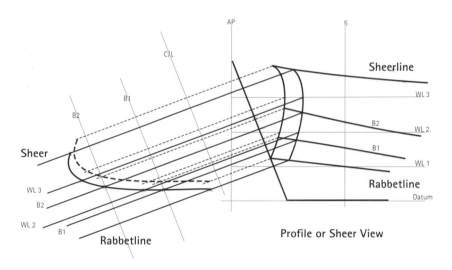

We have now finished with this form of Radiused Transom and can look at the second method, namely where the Radiused Transom is developed in the plane of the Waterlines.

LOFTING THE AFT FACE OF A RADIUSED TRANSOM, WHERE THE TRANSOM IS DEVELOPED IN THE PLANE OF THE WATERLINES

Step 1 (of 7) – using WL 3 as a worked example

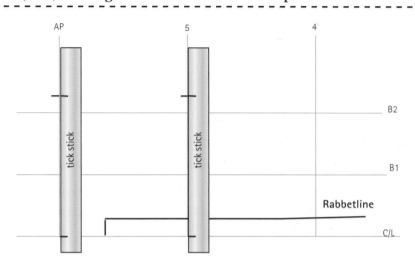

1   Lay the tick stick with the Half-breadth of WL 3, picked up in Step 4 of the common first stage, onto the AP, using the C/L as a reference.

2   Repeat this process for the next Station, in this case Stn 5.

Step 2

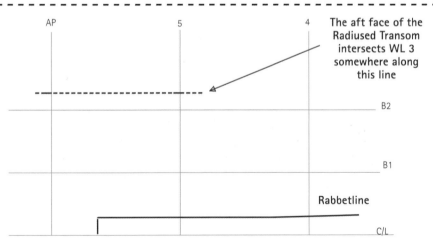

The aft face of the Radiused Transom intersects WL 3 somewhere along this line

1   Using a straight edge or ruler, join these two points together with a feint pencil line.

2   The actual Transom intersection for WL 3 lies somewhere along this line. To get the actual distance along the line, we'll need to look at WL 3 in the Sheer/Profile View.

Step 3

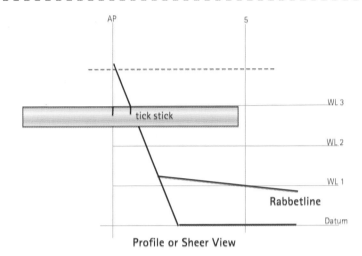

Profile or Sheer View

1 Lay a tick stick along WL 3 and pick up the AP and the intersection of the Transom C/L.

2 We'll then transfer this information to the Half-breadth View and scribe the Transom Radius for WL 3. This Radius information is usually found in either the Lines Plan or the offsets.

Step 4

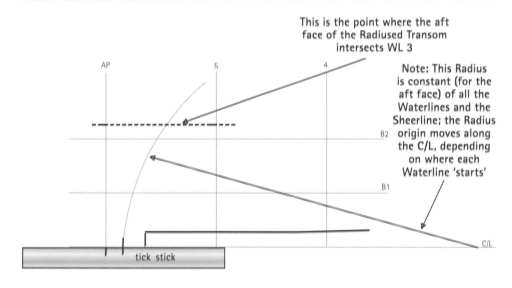

This is the point where the aft face of the Radiused Transom intersects WL 3

Note: This Radius is constant (for the aft face) of all the Waterlines and the Sheerline; the Radius origin moves along the C/L, depending on where each Waterline 'starts'

1 Lay the tick stick from Step 3 along the C/L, using the AP as a reference, and transfer the WL 3 information.

2 Using this mark, scribe a Radius arc until it intersects the line where WL 3 lies.

3 Where these two lines intersect is the aft face of the Radiused Transom at WL 3.

Step 5

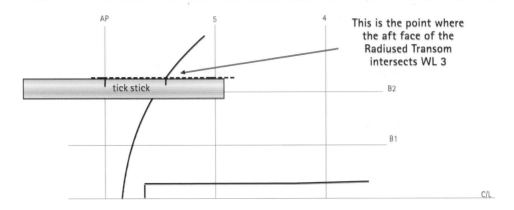

1 Lay a tick stick along the line as shown, and using the AP as a reference, pick up the intersection point of the Transom Radius with WL 3.

2 Transfer this information to the Profile View.

Step 6

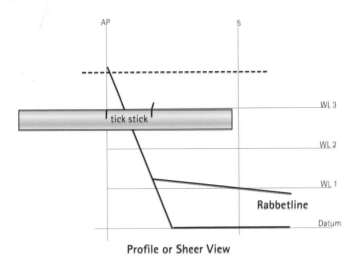

Profile or Sheer View

1 Lay a tick stick along WL 3, using the AP as a reference, and transfer the information picked up in Step 5 onto WL 3.

2 We now have the correct position for the aft face of the Radiused Transom at WL 3. Repeat this process for all of the remaining Waterlines and the Sheerline.

Step 7

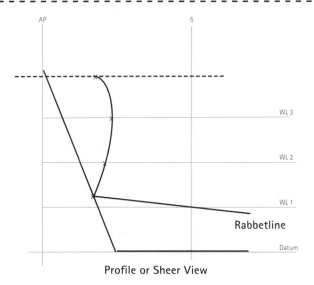

Profile or Sheer View

With all of the points plotted, we can now join them together with a flexible batten. This gives us the shape of the aft face of the Radiused Transom.

   We're now ready to plot the positions of the Transom/Buttock intersection points. To do this we'll use exactly the same techniques that we used earlier lofting the aft face of the other form of Radiused Transom, ie Steps 6, 7 and 8. We can then carry on lofting the boat, using these same techniques for lofting both a boat with a flat/raked Transom and a boat where the Transom is radiused perpendicular to the Transom angle.

The next section covers the techniques used to expand/develop the aft face of the Transom.

EXPANDING/DEVELOPING THE AFT FACE OF A RADIUSED TRANSOM, WHERE THE TRANSOM IS DEVELOPED IN THE PLANE OF THE WATERLINES

Step 1 (of 4) – using WL 3 as a worked example

As with the previous form of Radiused Transom, lines are drawn at 90 degrees to the angle of the Transom C/L, but they start at the intersection of the Radiused Transom and various lines (eg WL 3, B2 etc). We can also draw in an expansion C/L, but *not* B1 and B2, as will be explained later.

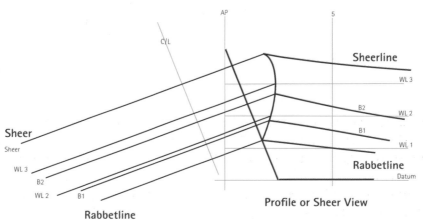

Profile or Sheer View

Step 2

1 Lay a flexible batten or tick stick around the Radius arc for WL 3 and pick up the C/L, B1, B2 and WL 3.

2 Transfer these points to the expanded Transom grid created previously.

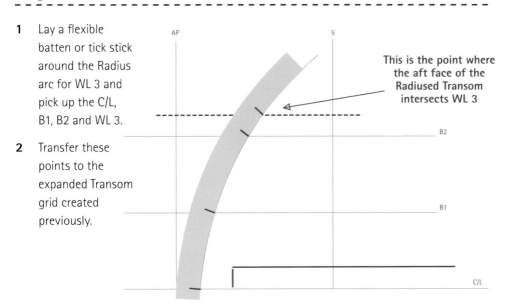

This is the point where the aft face of the Radiused Transom intersects WL 3

Step 3

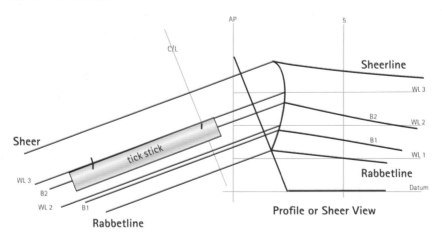

Taking WL 3 as a worked example, and using the C/L as a reference, unwrap the flexible batten/tick stick and transfer the curved Half-breadth, picked up in Step 2, onto the Transom expansion line as shown in the drawing.

Repeat this process for the remaining Waterlines, Buttock Lines, Sheerline and Rabbetline.

Step 4

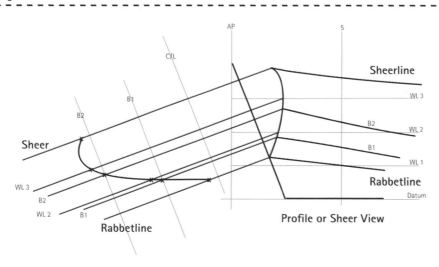

With all of the points plotted, use a flexible batten to develop the true 'expanded' aft face of the Radiused Transom.

In the next section, we move on to develop the forward face of the Transom; some of the techniques used are new but others are similar to ones used already.

EXPANDING/DEVELOPING THE FORWARD FACE OF A RADIUSED TRANSOM, WHERE THE TRANSOM IS DEVELOPED IN THE PLANE OF THE WATERLINES

We'll now look at the techniques used to develop/expand the forward face of a Radiused Transom, but, as before, this can't be done until the whole boat has been lofted.

Step 1 (of 9) – using WL 3 as a worked example

As with a flat/raked Transom, draw a line parallel to the Transom C/L, but forward of it by the thickness of the Transom, and extend the line down to the Radius C/L.

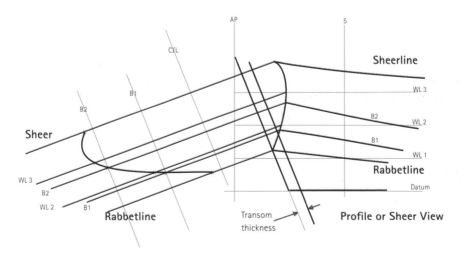

Step 2

1   Lay a tick stick along WL 3, using the AP as a reference, and pick up the forward face of the 'Transom thickness'. As you can see from the drawing, this 'length' is 'measured' along WL 3, not perpendicular to the Transom angle.

2   Transfer this information to the Half-breadth View.

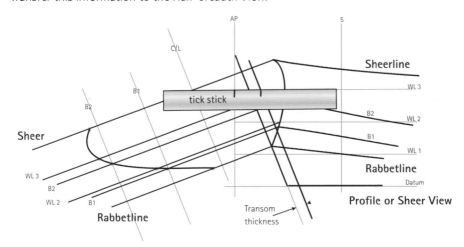

Step 3

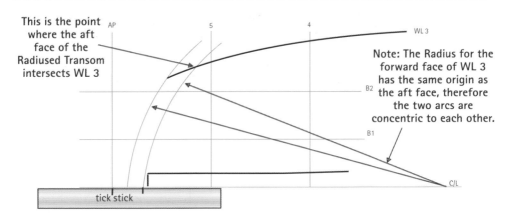

This is the point where the aft face of the Radiused Transom intersects WL 3

Note: The Radius for the forward face of WL 3 has the same origin as the aft face, therefore the two arcs are concentric to each other.

1 Lay the tick stick along the C/L, using the AP as a reference, and transfer the information picked up in Step 2.

2 Using this mark, scribe a Radius arc until it intersects the line where WL 3 lies.

3 Where these two lines intersect is the forward face of the Radiused Transom at WL 3.

Step 4

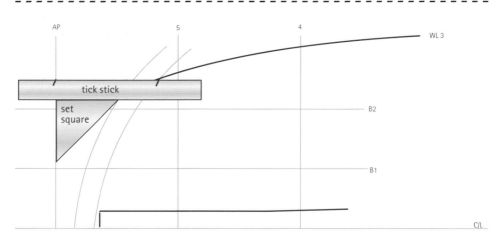

1 Using a set square to ensure that the tick stick is aligned in a truly horizontal manner, pick up the AP and the intersection point of WL 3 with the forward face of the Transom Radius, as shown in the drawing.

2 Transfer this information to the Profile View.

Step 5

1   Lay the tick stick along WL 3, using the AP as a reference, and transfer the forward face of the Radiused Transom, picked up in Step 4, onto WL 3, as shown in the drawing.

2   Repeat this process for the remaining Waterlines, the Sheerline and the Rabbetline. (For clarity, the existing lines/development of the aft face are shown as dotted lines.)

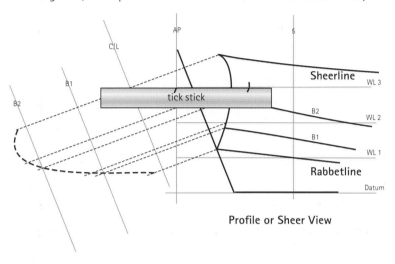

Profile or Sheer View

Step 6

1   With the forward face of the Transom plotted in the Profile View, we can now project lines at 90 degrees to the Radiused Transom's C/L, where the forward face of the Transom intersects with the Sheerline, Rabbetline, Buttocks and Waterlines.

2   As with the previous Transom, the lines of the forward face are parallel to, but below the lines of, the aft face.

3   We can now pick up the Radius intersection points, from the Half-breadth View, and 'unwrap' them along their respective lines.

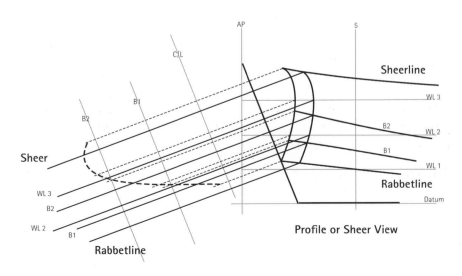

Profile or Sheer View

123

Step 7

1 Lay a flexible batten or tick stick around the Radius arc (for the forward face) as shown in the drawing above. Mark on the C/L and the intersection of the Radius with WL 3.

2 Transfer these points to the Profile View.

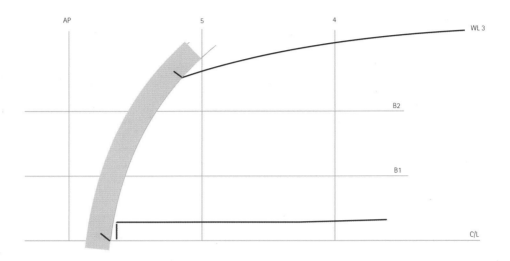

Step 8

1 Using the C/L as a reference, unwrap the flexible batten/tick stick and transfer the curved Half-breadth, picked up in Step 7, onto the Transom expansion line as shown in the drawing.

2 Repeat this process for the remaining Waterlines, Buttock Lines, Sheerline and Rabbetline.

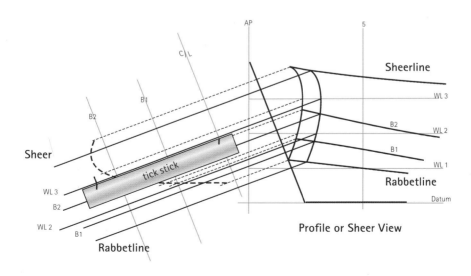

Step 9

With all of the points plotted, use a flexible batten to develop the true 'expanded' forward face of the Radiused Transom.

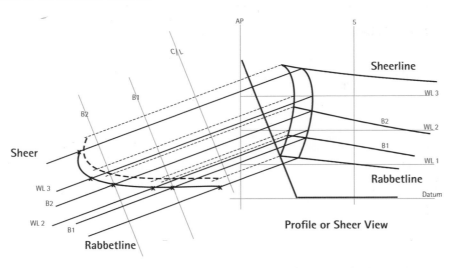

Profile or Sheer View

This is the end of the main lofting techniques, and we'll now move on to the areas that will help in the eventual construction of the boat.

MOVING ON FROM THE LOFTING

With the major parts of the lofting completed, we can now move on to creating cross-sections for the Keel and the Stem. These cross-sections are needed to turn the full-size lofting into an actual boat!

We'll start with the Keel cross-sections, as they are the easier to create, and then move on to the Stem Bevel cross-sections, which involve some transferring of lengths etc but will use techniques that you're already fully familiar with.

When we're creating these cross-sections, we'll need to use the 'Scantlings' of the boat to ensure we're building it to the designer's specification. 'Scantlings' are a boatbuilding term for 'sizes': for instance, the frame of a yacht may have Scantlings of 1in (25mm) Moulding x 2in (50mm) Siding. As a general rule, the 'Moulding' is a measurement from the inside of a boat outwards, and the other is the 'Siding'. As an illustration of this, consider the following deck beam – it has a Moulding of 3in (75mm) and a Siding of 2in (50mm).

In most cases, the Moulding and Siding are easy to distinguish, but in a few areas it may take a bit of thought to figure out which is which.

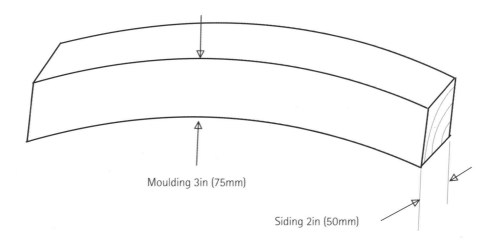

Moulding 3in (75mm)

Siding 2in (50mm)

KEEL CROSS-SECTIONS AND BEVEL BOARD

Step 1 (of 8)

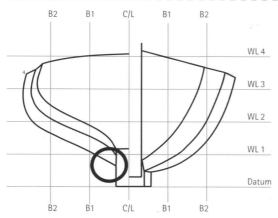

We're starting with the Keel cross-sections, as they are generally easier to understand and therefore give a foundation to build on when we come to the Stem Bevel cross-sections. The Keel or Keel/Hog cross-sections use the Body Plan that we lofted earlier. For clarity, we're only going to do one Keel cross-section, as the technique is then repeated for all the others, and we'll look at the cross-section of Stn 4, concentrating on the area that is circled in the drawing.

Step 2

1   We'll assume that this particular boat has hull planking that is ¾in (20mm) thick, and that, where possible, we'll draw the cross-section so that it complies with Lloyd's Rules.

2   Perpendicular from Stn 4, draw a series of marks projecting inwards for ¾in (20mm) and then join them together with a line, which represents the inside of the hull planking – as mentioned before, the assumption is that the lofting is to the outside of the hull, therefore the planking 'thickness' will be drawn 'inboard' of the Station Lines.

3   Where Stn 4 meets the Rabbetline, project a solid line perpendicular to the Station which will then join with the inside of the hull planking line as shown in the drawing .

127

Step 3

1 This intersection point is variously known as the Ghost Line, Middle Line, Inner Rabbet, Middle Rabbet and probably lots more that I'm unaware of, but I'll be referring to it as the Ghost Line – old habits die hard!

2 With this particular lofting the Ghost Line is where the Keel and Hog join, as you'll see shortly, but if you're lofting a 'deep-keeled' cruising boat, then it may not necessarily have a Hog.

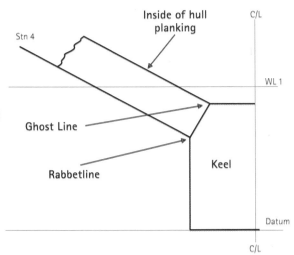

3 Draw a line out horizontally from the Ghost Line until it meets the C/L.

4 The 'shape' below this line is the half section of the Keel, and we can now look at drawing in the Hog.

Step 4

1 From the Scantlings, find the 'Moulding' of the Hog, in this case its thickness, and measure vertically up the C/L from the top of the Keel.

2 From the top of the Hog, measure out, from the C/L, by the half Siding of the Hog – the reason for using the half Siding is that this cross-section shows the Moulding in full but only half of the Siding, as it is symmetrical about the C/L.

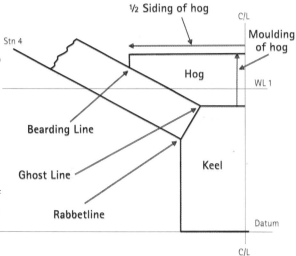

3 Return a line vertically down from this point until it touches the inside of the hull planking – this point is known as the 'Bearding Line' or 'Bearding' – to comply with Lloyd's Rules, the distance from the Ghost Line to the Bearding Line needs to be at least twice the planking thickness.

4 Repeat this process for all of the other Stations in the Body Plan.

Step 5

With all of the Keel cross-sections completed, the Body Plan will look very 'confused', with many of the cross-sections overlapping each other; therefore it's a good idea to make a Bevel Board which contains all of the relevant information for each Station in table form. For the sake of clarity, all unnecessary information has been removed from the drawing, leaving only what is needed to help create the Bevel Board.

Draw a series of lines as shown in the drawing. Note that when we take any measurements they'll be drawn 'outwards' from either the C/L or the 'Join Line'. The actual Moulding size won't be used, because if we were to use it and the Moulding dimension of the actual Keel or Hog larger or smaller than it was meant to be, it would adversely affect the size of points B, C etc and the relationship between them, thereby giving us an incorrect set of information from which to build the boat.

We can now take measurements from these cross-sections and put them into a Bevel Board.

Step 6

Using a tape measure or ruler, take the measurements A to E and put them into a Bevel Board table. The Bevel Board is typically made out of an offcut of plywood, or similar, as it is less likely to get thrown away accidentally than if it were done on a piece of paper.

We can take the measurements in either metric or imperial – what matters is that you can read and understand the measurements you have taken. I tend to use imperial for larger dimensions and metric for smaller dimensions – eg a yacht may be 30ft long but the galley locker may have a width of 300mm.

The following page shows a typical form of Bevel Board/Table (see Step 7). This information is used to create a construction drawing from which the boat's 'Backbone' is built.

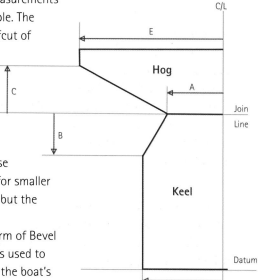

Step 7

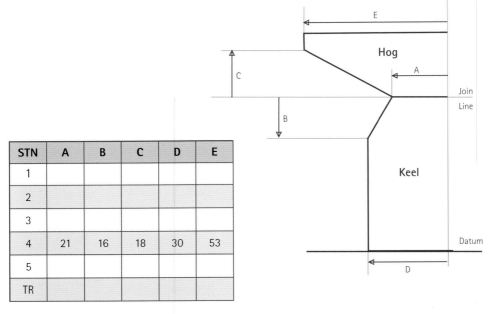

STN	A	B	C	D	E
1					
2					
3					
4	21	16	18	30	53
5					
TR					

Keel/Hog Bevel Board (all dimensions in mm)

Step 8

We've now completed the Bevel Board for the Keel/Hog cross-section; as we saw in Step 6, this information is used when we actually build the boat, and the Bevel Board, along with all the templates, laminating jigs etc, form the starting point.

We're now going to look at the techniques used to draw the cross-sections of the Stem, also known as Stem Bevel Development. The most accurate way to develop the Stem cross-sections is by drawing a series of cross-sections developed around the curve of the Stem, and then, as with the Keel/Hog, we can record the information on a Bevel Board. The method used is slightly involved, but once again we'll cover what needs to be done gradually.

STEM CROSS-SECTIONS AND BEVEL BOARD

Step 1 (of 11)

Using a straight edge, draw a line at 90 degrees to the curve of the Stem/Rabbetline. Because the curve is not constant this will need to be an educated guess – trust your eye when drawing this line! We'll then need to find the Half-breadth of all the points that this line crosses, ie Rabbetline, Waterlines and Buttock Lines.

Next we'll 'expand' the Half-breadths to one side of the line, giving us a half cross-section. The Buttock Lines are a known Half-breadth and some people advocate just using these and ignoring the Waterlines, but this would be a mistake as you wouldn't get the true shape of the cross-section.

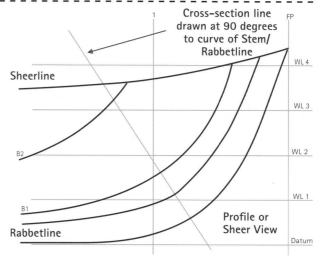

Step 2

1 As explained in Step 1, the Buttocks have a known Half-breadth, so it is relatively easy to plot them along the line. All developments will be perpendicular to the line we've drawn.

2 For the sake of clarity, we'll look at developing the lines that are circled in the drawing, ie Rabbetline, B1 and WL 2. The techniques required for the other lines (WL 3 and B2) are exactly the same.

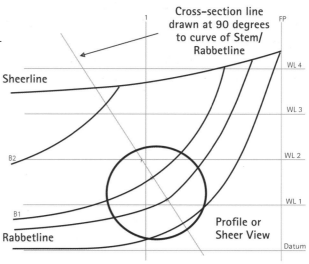

Step 3

1. Using a set square, draw lines projecting out from the points as shown in the drawing.

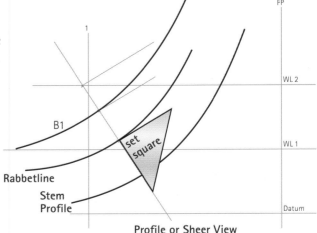

Profile or Sheer View

2. The Half-breadth of B1 is a known constant quantity, so it is simply a case of using a tick stick to pick up the Half-breadth of B1 from either the Body Plan or the Half-breadth View – a technique you have used many times before – and transferring it to the line that we've just drawn.

We will now look at the technique used to find the correct Half-breadth of the Waterlines and/or the Rabbetline.

Step 4

We now need to find the Half-breadth of WL 2 where it intersects the Stem cross-section line.

1. Lay a tick stick along WL 2, using the FP as a reference, and pick up the intersection point with the Stem cross-section line.

2. Transfer this information to the Half-breadth View, and we'll determine the true Half-breadth of WL 2 at this position.

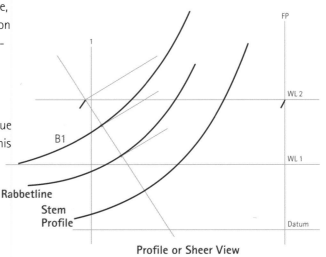

Profile or Sheer View

Step 5

1 Lay the tick stick along the C/L, using the FP as a reference, and transfer the intersection point picked up in Step 4 onto the C/L.

2 Repeat this process using one of the Buttock Lines – as we saw previously, the further apart these reference points are spaced, the more accurate the final line will be.

3 Next, we will join these two points together with a feint line.

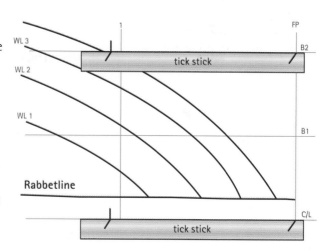

Step 6

Using a straight edge or ruler, join these two points together with a feint pencil line. Where this line intersects WL 2 is the correct Half-breadth of WL 2 in the Stem cross-section we drew earlier. We'll then pick up and transfer this information to the Stem cross-section.

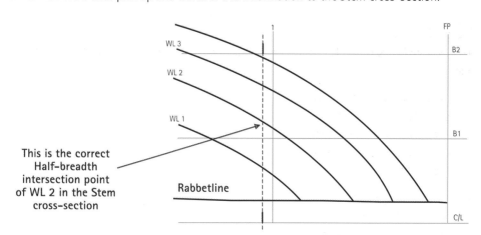

This is the correct Half-breadth intersection point of WL 2 in the Stem cross-section

Step 7

1 Lay a tick stick vertically along the line as shown in the drawing.

2 Using the C/L as a reference, pick up the Half-breadth of WL 2.

3 Transfer this information back to the Profile View, where it can be plotted on the Stem cross-section.

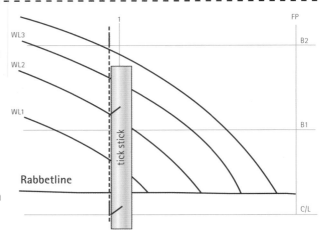

Step 8

1 Lay the tick stick along the cross-section line as shown in the drawing and transfer the information picked up in Step 7.

2 Repeat this process for the remaining Waterlines, Buttocks and Rabbetline.

3 With all of the points plotted, we can now join them together to show the true shape of the cross-section.

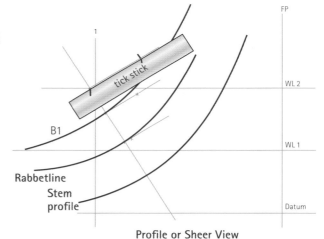

Profile or Sheer View

Step 9

1 Using a flexible batten, join together the points to show the shape of the cross-section.

2 Repeat this process at other points around the curve of the Stem – typically around 6–8 cross-sections are made to give an accurate picture of the change in cross-section of the Stem.

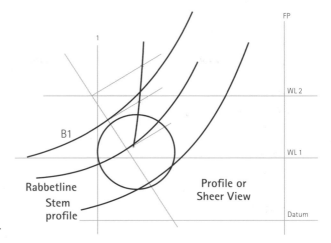

3 We're now ready to use this information to create a Stem Bevel Board (see Step 10).

4 As with the Keel Bevel Board, we'll concentrate on the area circled.

Step 10

1 The Stem/Apron cross-section is drawn in exactly the same way as the Keel/Hog cross-section, and when it's finished we'll end up with a cross-section drawing very similar – depending on the individual proportions of the boat – to that shown here.

2 When all of the cross-sections have been completed, we can then make a Stem Bevel Board showing a similar-looking set of data to that produced for the Keel/Hog.

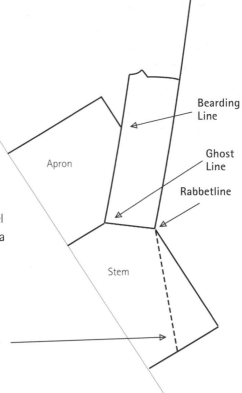

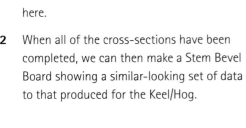

The dashed line shows how the front of the Stem is typically finished, rather than leaving it square, to give a finer entry through the water

Step 11

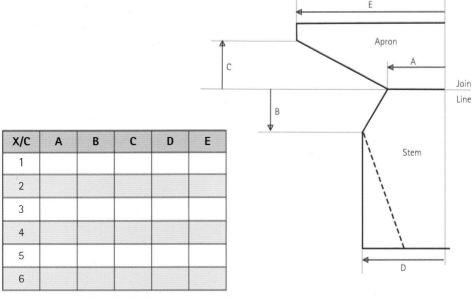

X/C	A	B	C	D	E
1					
2					
3					
4					
5					
6					

Stem/Apron Bevel Board (all dimensions in mm)

FINAL TECHNIQUES

With both Bevel Boards complete, we can now look at how we can account for planking thickness at the Transom and also at the Stations in the Body Plan – with a boat that is lofted to the outside of the hull, we need to 'take off' the planking thickness *before* we make the Mould Station/building Mould. We'll focus on two different techniques for doing this, followed by a brief look at their relative merits.

When we make a Mould Station we need to allow for the change in size of the Mould Station, depending upon the thickness of material used to actually make the Mould. We'll look at a very simple technique that allows us to make a Frame/Station Bevel Board and accommodate almost any thickness of material used to build the Mould.

Finally, we'll take a brief look at a simple but effective technique for taking templates or patterns off the loft floor.

Before we start with accounting for planking thickness, and for this we'll be looking at a Station taken at random from within the Body Plan ...

ACCOUNTING FOR PLANKING THICKNESS AT MOULD STATIONS

Step 1 (of 6)

1   The first technique, and arguably the easiest, is simply to use a pair of compasses to draw a series of arcs – where the Radius of the arc is the same as the planking thickness – around the curve of the Station, as shown in the drawing.

2   Join the 'top' of these arcs together with a line which then represents the inside of the hull planking.

3   It can be argued that this technique is too simple and doesn't work as accurately when a boat has a pronounced change in shape or curvature. We'll discuss these differences *after* looking at the second technique.

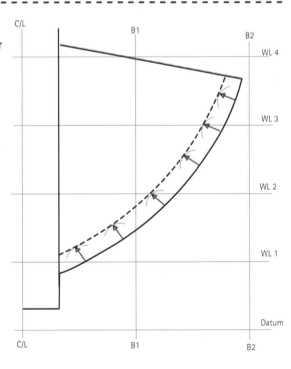

Step 2

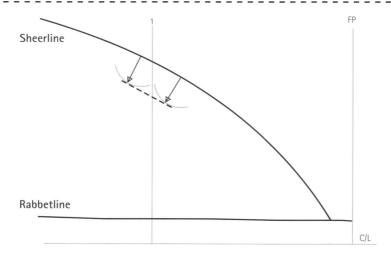

1   For clarity, only the lines relevant to the technique are shown. Again, using a pair of compasses draw two arcs either side of the Station Line. Make these arcs as close to the Station Line as possible – if they are too far apart, the resulting measurement won't be accurate.

2   Join these two arcs together with a feint line.

3   We'll now take a measurement along the Station Line and transfer it to the Body Plan.

Step 3

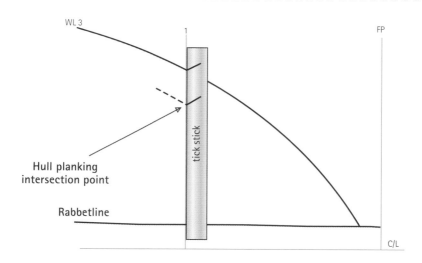

1   Lay the tick stick on Stn 1 and pick up the intersection with WL 3 and the 'dashed' line that represents the planking thickness.

2   We'll now transfer this information to the Body Plan and plot onto Stn 1/WL 3.

Step 4

1   Lay the tick stick, as shown in the drawing, so that it lies at 90 degrees to the curve of the Station Line – as before, trust your eye as a guide to when the tick stick is aligned at 90 degrees – and the two intersection points are touching both the Body Plan Station Line and the Waterline, in this case WL 3.

2   Repeat this process for the remaining Waterlines and the Sheerline.

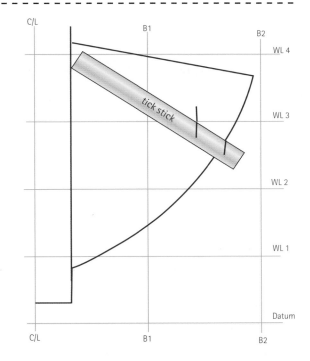

Step 5

We now have a series of points that can be joined together to show the inside of the hull planking. As you can see, this method has less points for each Station but the process is more involved – in terms of accuracy, there's always going to be the issue of aligning the tick stick correctly at 90 degrees to the Station curve; even if we were to use a set square, absolute accuracy couldn't be guaranteed.

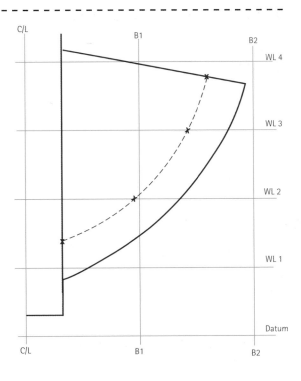

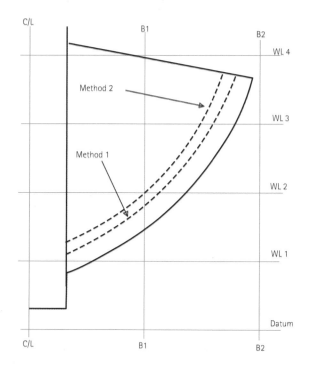

A comparison of the two methods generally shows that the first method reduces the Station Mould size slightly less than the second method. This can have considerable advantages when it comes to actually making the building Moulds: method 1 will usually give us a slightly larger building Mould and, as my Dad has always said, 'it's easier to take wood off than it is to add wood on'.

Again, in practice, building Moulds are usually made of softwood and will naturally expand and contract irrespective of how 'perfectly' we may have made them in the first place.

CREATING A FRAME/STATION BEVEL BOARD, USING STN 1 AS A WORKED EXAMPLE

Step 1 (of 4)

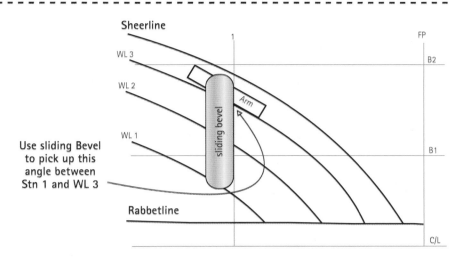

Sheerline

WL 3

WL 2

WL 1

FP

B2

B1

Use sliding Bevel
to pick up this
angle between
Stn 1 and WL 3

sliding bevel

Arm

Rabbetline

C/L

1 Using an adjustable/sliding Bevel, lay the 'body' of the Bevel on Stn 1 and adjust the 'sliding arm' so that it follows the curve of the Waterline, in this case WL 3.

2 Lock the Bevel arm in place and transfer this information to a Bevel Board.

Step 2

1 Lay the sliding Bevel against the edge of the Bevel Board. The edge used must be straight to ensure that all of the angles transferred over from the Station are set out to a common reference.

2 Copy this angle onto the board with a pencil and extend it, as shown in the drawing, if necessary.

3 Repeat this process for the remaining Waterlines at the Station or Frame.

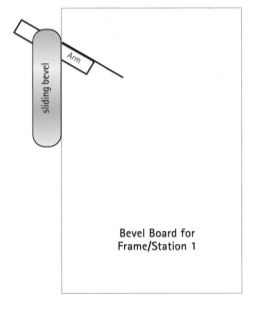

sliding bevel

Arm

Bevel Board for
Frame/Station 1

Step 3

1 With all of the Station Bevels plotted onto the board, it should look similar to the drawing. As we can see, the angle is different, depending on the angle at which the Waterline crossed the Station.

2 We can now construct a line which is parallel to the reference edge and is the same size as either the frame 'Siding' or the thickness of material being used to construct the building Mould. For the sake of argument, let's say that the wood is going to be 20mm (¾in) thick.

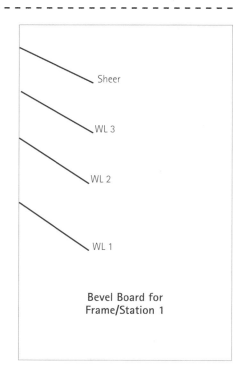

Bevel Board for
Frame/Station 1

Step 4

1 Draw a line, as shown in the drawing, parallel to the reference edge of the Bevel Board.

2 At each point that it intersects an angled line, draw a line back to the reference edge.

3 The 'gap' created is the amount of material that will need to be removed from the narrow side of the Mould Station.

Remove this amount. Depends upon angle, material thickness etc

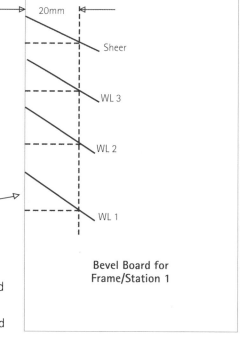

Bevel Board for
Frame/Station 1

All that is needed now is to record the information so that it does not get lost, rubbed out or painted over.

The final topic deals with the basic method of picking up a template or shape off the loft floor.

PICKING UP PATTERNS/TEMPLATES OFF THE LOFT FLOOR

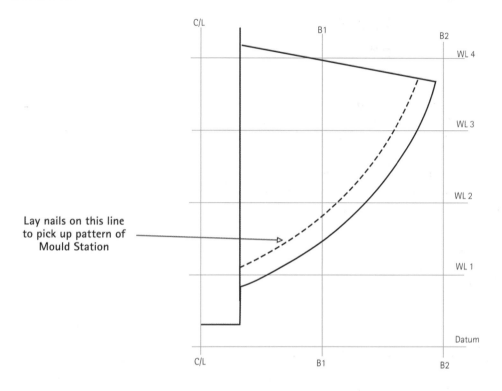

Lay nails on this line to pick up pattern of Mould Station

1 Lay a series of nails on the loft floor so that they follow the pattern that we want to copy.

2 The nails have had part of their head filed or ground away so that they sit on the loft floor without rolling.

3 With the nails in position, a piece of wood is pressed over the nails and a series of nail marks are transferred to the wood. This may seem a crude way of making a template or pattern, particularly in this day of CAD software, but it has worked well for many years – if a technique works, why change it?

BASIC LOFTING GLOSSARY

Aft Perpendicular (AP)
A vertical line in the Profile View that defines the back of the boat

Backbone
The structural members that make up the spine, or Backbone, of the boat

Bevel Board
A board showing the angle at which one surface meets another: for example, the angle at which the planking intersects the Mould Station

Body Plan
The area of the Lines Drawing that shows the boat as a series of vertical cross-sections

Buttock Lines (B)
These are straight lines in the Body Plan and the Half-breadth View set out parallel to the centreline (C/L). In the Profile View, Buttocks appear as curved lines, drawn using information taken from two different sources – the Body Plan and the Half-breadth View – and are used to carry out the initial fairing of the boat

Camber/Deck Camber
The curved surface to the top of the deck which sheds water and reduces the risk of the deck structure collapsing because of loading put on it

Centreline (C/L)
A line in both the Body Plan and the Half-breadth View where any Half-breadths, or widths, are referenced from

Datum or Baseline
A horizontal line in the Profile View and the Body Plan that can act as a reference for all of the Waterlines drawn on the Lofting Grid

Diagonals (D)
These lines appear as 'angled' straight lines in the Body Plan that will ideally cut through the curve of the Station at right angles. They are curved lines in the Half-breadth and are used to check the fairness of all the other lines

Forward Perpendicular (FP)
A vertical line in the Profile View that defines the front of the boat

Half-breadth View
A series of horizontal half cross-sections – viewed from above or below the boat – drawn along the boat's Waterlines

Keel
The principal structural member of a wooden boat

Lines Drawing
The various views of the boat, consisting of the Body Plan, Profile and Half-breadth Views

Lofting Grid
This is the basic layout of Datum, Station Lines, Waterlines and Buttock Lines used to loft our boat onto. The size and spacing of the Lofting Grid will be different for each boat, but the 'grid' principle is the same

Mould
A temporary frame used to define the cross-sectional shape of the boat at a certain point

Profile View

The area of the Lines Drawing that shows the Profile or side view of the boat

Rabbetline

This is the line where the hull planking ends at the Stem or Keel

Radiused Transom

A Transom which is curved, or radiused, it is also typically raked and is usually found on an elegant yacht rather than a working boat

Scantlings

A boatbuilding term for the size(s) of a boat's constructional members

Sheerline (Sheer)

This line is basically the top of the hull and plays a great part in determining how the final boat will look

Station Lines (Stns)

In the Profile View and Half-breadth View they are vertical spacings typically measured from the FP aft. In the Body Plan, the Station Lines are a series of cross-sections

Stem

The structural Backbone member at the forward end of the boat

Transom

The 'flat' section at the aft of the boat where the planking ends; it can be vertical or raked back at an angle, depending on the design

Tumblehome

A situation where the Sheer is not the widest point for any given cross-section, ie the hull shape comes back on itself

Waterlines (WL)

Horizontal lines in both the Profile View and the Body Plan set out at spacings determined by the designer or naval architect. In the Half-breadth View, the Waterlines are a series of curved lines running fore and aft

INDEX